MORE EVERYDAY PRAYERS

MORE EVERYDAY PRAYERS

Contributors
HENRY McKEATING
JOHN REARDON
MICHAEL WALKER

Editor
HAZEL SNASHALL

INTERNATIONAL BIBLE READING ASSOCIATION
National Christian Education Council
Robert Denholm House
Nutfield, Redhill, Surrey, RH1 4HW

ACKNOWLEDGEMENTS

We are grateful for permission to include the following:

Verses from the *New English Bible*, © 1970 (Oxford and Cambridge University Presses);

John Wesley's Covenant Prayer from *The Methodist Service Book* (Methodist Publishing House) on page 48;

Extract from *Marked for Life* by Maria Boulding (SPCK) on page 60.

Biblical quotations are from the *New English Bible* unless otherwise indicated.

Cover photograph by Martin Snashall

ISBN 0-7197-0325-5

Typeset by Solo Typesetting, Maidstone, Kent
Printed and bound by Lonsdale Universal Printing Ltd, Bath, Avon

CONTENTS

INTRODUCTION

Few people find it easy to sustain their prayer life without some help. This book of prayers and meditations is designed to give such help by suggesting a theme for each day over a period of two months, together with prayers for the special days of the Christian year and for many common human experiences.

The pattern for each day varies but usually includes thanksgiving to God and supplication and intercession for our needs. To focus thought and meditation, use is made of biblical passages and some of the hymns of the church.

Whilst personal need and preference will influence the use of this book, it is suggested that time is given for silent meditation and reflection so that the words of the prayers may become a springboard for personal and private prayers.

Here is a guide to daily prayer written out of the wide-ranging and distinctive experiences of the three contributors—the Revd Dr Henry McKeating, a Methodist Minister; the Revd John Reardon, a Minister of the United Reformed Church; and the Revd Michael Walker, a Baptist Minister.

SHARING THE COMMON LIFE

SHARING THE DAYS

Family **Day 1**

I am reminded of the sincerity of your faith, a faith which was alive in Lois your grandmother and Eunice your mother before you, and which, I am confident, lives in you also. *(2 Timothy 1.5)*

Father, how can I express what I owe to my family?
I have shared so much of life with them, old and young.
Even when they are far from me, we are bound closely together.
When I am angry or frustrated, they rescue me from myself;
when I doubt, they rekindle my faith.
My family make demands on my time and my energy;
they remind me that I am still wanted.

Father, I thank you for family life:
for the routines of the home,
for laughter and conversation,
for arguments and agreements,
for play and relaxation,
for every glimpse of your love in our closeness to one another.

Father, forgive me for every time when I have wanted to turn from my family, to give way to selfishness, to overlook the needs of others. So often they look to me for maturity and wisdom, and they find pettiness; they expect generosity, and they find meanness; they depend on me and I let them down.

Father, from whom every family receives its true name,
I pray for all the members of my family:
for those who are growing up,
that they may increase in wisdom and love;
for those facing changes,
that they may meet them with hope;
for those who are weak,
that they may find strength;
for those with heavy burdens,
that they may carry them lightly;
for those who are old and frail,
that they may grow in faith.

Strangers

Day 2

When I was a stranger you took me into your home. *(Matthew 25.35)*

God, our Father, you have often come to us as a stranger, but we have not recognised you. Yet how often has the word of a stranger helped us, challenged us or comforted us.

We thank you for times when we were lost and were shown the way by a stranger, when we were being foolish and a stranger brought us to our senses, when we were weary and were given refreshment by someone we did not know. Your Holy Spirit was with us in those moments making life more rich and abundant.

Father, we think of the lost opportunities,
when we saw someone in trouble and did not go to help them,
when our shyness stopped us from speaking a friendly word,
when prejudice created a barrier against those who are different.
We hear the words of Jesus, 'Anything you did not do for one of these, however humble, you did not do for me.' Open our eyes to recognise Christ in the strangers who continually offer us a chance to cross the chasms of mistrust, suspicion and fear, to make community.

We pray for the strangers in our society,
for young people who have left home to study or to work,
for others who have deliberately left no traces
and who have hidden themselves far from home,
for foreigners with few personal friends,
for those who have been in prison,
for those who have adopted a life of wandering,
for the lonely and those whose closest friends and relations have died.

Father, there are many who want us to take refuge in prejudice and to believe that people with different styles of life and different faiths are inferior. Save us from all that hinders the free movement of your Holy Spirit, from suspicion, from fear, from false pride, so that our lives may be open to all whom you send us, friend and stranger alike.

There is no greater love than this, that a man should lay down his life for his friends. *(John 15.13)*

One there is above all others
Well deserves the name of Friend,
His is love beyond a brother's,
Costly, free, and knows no end. *John Newton*

Lord, where would we be without our friends?
They give us of themselves unselfishly,
they stand by us in trouble,
in happiness they share our laughter;
they make life more colourful.

Make me a good friend,
ready to help, but not to interfere,
loyal, but not uncritical,
open, rather than exclusive,
dependable at all times.

Lord Jesus Christ, you have not only given yourself as friend to all God's people, you have taught us what true friendship is. You mixed with the outcasts and sinners, sharing their celebrations, and yet never betrayed your Father. You crossed the road to greet and to touch the sick when everyone else hurried past in fear. Even when you were tired, you stopped to encourage those who waited for your blessing. You fearlessly exposed the hypocrisy of those who came seeking your support for their prejudices, but you were gentle with those who came seeking the truth. Above all, you gave your life that all God's people might know him as Father and you as friend and Saviour.

Pray for your friends by name, thinking of their special needs.

Teach me, Lord, what it means to lay down my life for my friends.

Colleagues

We must not be conceited, challenging one another to rivalry, jealous of one another. If a man should do something wrong, my brothers, on a sudden impulse, you who are endowed with the Spirit must set him right again very gently. Look to yourself, each one of you: you may be tempted too. Help one another to carry these heavy loads, and in this way you will fulfil the law of Christ. (Galatians 5.26 to 6.2)

Father, I share my life with many people
but few are as close as those who work with me.
I praise you for the support they give me,
and for the responsibilities we share.
I thank you for times when they have saved me from serious mistakes
and for the fellowship of common service.
Forgive me for times when I have been stubborn,
refusing to accept the good advice of others
or the new insights of those junior to me.
Forgive me for selfish ambition
and foolish thoughts of my own importance.
Forgive me for careless words when under pressure
and for failing to appreciate the needs of others for encouragement and praise.

Pray for close colleagues by name
Through our work together, Lord, may we contribute to your loving purposes for the world. May we serve others so that life for them may be fuller and richer.

Pray for those who are unemployed or retired
Father, I pray for those who have no paid employment and who have no colleagues, that they may not despair but may find other ways of working for the well-being of society and may find fellowship in common enterprise. Bless those whose days of retirement have separated them from colleagues and give them a sense of their continuing worth as your children. Enlarge our experience of community life that we may see each other as fellow-workers in your wider kingdom, because we all belong to one another in Christ.

Jesus said, 'Let the children come to me; do not try to stop them; for the kingdom of Heaven belongs to such as these.'

(Matthew 19.14)

When I see children, Father,
I am taken back to the pleasures and pains
of my own childhood.
Thank you for the love of my parents,
and the devotion of my teachers.
I remember the happy times with friends and family,
and I recall how I sometimes learnt the hard way and cried.
So many people shared their lives with me as I grew up,
and they are still part of me.
May their influence continue to work in me for good,
making my life a reflection of the love so freely given.

When I see children, Father,
I hope for the future,
that it may be full of laughter and purpose,
that it may be peaceful and just.

So I pray, Father, for today's children,
that they may be surrounded by love;
that they may grow in wisdom and faith;
that they may learn to be open with one another;
that they may care for your world;
that they may be generous in their concern for others.

I pray for parents, teachers, club leaders and all adults,
that they may nurture our children with tenderness
and firmness;
that they may know when to say yes and when to say no;
and that they may be as quick to learn as to teach.

The disciples came to Jesus and asked, 'Who is the greatest in the kingdom of Heaven?' He called a child, set him in front of them, and said, 'I tell you this: unless you turn round and become like children, you will never enter the kingdom of Heaven.' *(Matthew 18.1-3)*

Those who serve us

Day 6

There are varieties of gifts, but the same Spirit.
There are varieties of service, but the same Lord.
(1 Corinthians 12.4-5)

So many people work for me
to meet my needs
to enrich my life.
Father, I pray for them all:
those I meet and know,
those I see but do not greet,
the many I do not see and take for granted.

I give thanks, Lord, for the development of human society,
with all the interactions between people;
for the binding of our lives together,
through our work, through public services,
through communications and through leisure.

Forgive me, Father, for my self-centred concerns,
for judging people unkindly without any regard for them,
for expecting too much of hard-pressed strangers,
for accepting service without returning any warmth.

I pray for those whose lives are spent in serving others:
the public officials in local government,
shopworkers, bank clerks and postmen,
craftsmen and factory workers,
librarians and teachers,
social workers, doctors and nurses,
police and traffic wardens,
and a host of others too numerous to name.
Lord God, as I meet them today, or use their services, awaken in me a grateful and gracious response, that their offering of themselves may not be wasted, but may increase in value as I offer it to you.

But you are a chosen race, a royal priesthood, a dedicated nation, and a people claimed by God for his own, to proclaim the triumphs of him who has called you out of darkness into his marvellous light. You are now the people of God, who once were not his people; outside his mercy once, you have now received his mercy. (1 Peter 2.9-10)

Holy Spirit of God, bind us to one another in love and trust within the fellowship of the church. Make us faithful witnesses to your goodness, fearless proclaimers of your truth, and humble seekers of your continuing guidance.

I pray for the members of my local congregation:
for all who lead in worship,
for those who administer property and funds,
for young people and children and all who lead them,
for frail and elderly members and those who visit them,
for all whose ministry is in the secular sphere.
Keep us open to one another as we share life together,
but keep us open to others, welcoming and accepting.
Through our common life
let us hear your living word in our worship,
and probe its meaning in our study;
confirm our faith through prayer,
and test it in action;
enlarge our hope as we encourage each other;
deepen our love as we share the gospel,
and broaden it as we offer it to the world.

O Sovereign Lord, Almighty God, look upon thy Church and upon all thy people, and save us all, the sheep of thy flock. Give us thy peace, and thy love, and thy help, and send down upon us the free gift of thy Holy Spirit; that we may be united in the bond of peace and love, one body and one spirit; in one faith, as we have been called in one hope of our calling; through Jesus Christ our Lord, with whom, and with the Holy Spirit, thou art blessed for evermore. Amen

(Liturgy of St Mark)

Joy **Day 8**

Give me joy in my heart, keep me praising

Father, there is so much to be joyful about:
the natural world around us,
infinitely varied, beautiful, and ever new,
the comforts of modern life,
the closeness of others in family and friendship,
the many opportunities for helping others,
the fresh experience and the secure routine.

Give me joy in my heart, I pray

Dear God, let me show my joy,
by encouraging those who are unsure of themselves,
by helping those who are weak,
by laughing with those who are happy,
and by sharing faith with those who search for truth.

Give me joy in my heart, keep me praising

God, our Father, we rejoice in your love
made known to us in Jesus Christ.
He died for us while we were yet sinners
and with him we are raised to eternal life
through the power and the love of your Holy Spirit.
We know, through the teaching of Jesus, that you value us;
that even the hairs on our heads are numbered
and that you know us by name.
Through him, also, we know that we are forgiven,
set free from our sins and given a new start in life.
Above all, we know that your love can never be exhausted;
that nothing can stand in its way;
that nothing can keep it from us.

Keep me praising till the break of day

I cry aloud to the Lord;
to the Lord I plead aloud for mercy.
I pour out my complaint before him
and tell over my troubles in his presence.
(Psalm 142.1-2)

Today I want to indulge myself,
to grieve for the lost opportunities,
the near misses and the outright failures.
So often I fall short of my own goals,
and sometimes I even forget I have set them.
Father, forgive me for my weaknesses:
for being obstinate when I should give way,
for submitting when I should stand firm,
for judging when I should be forgiving,
for being pessimistic instead of hopeful.

I cry to thee, O Lord,
and say, 'Thou art my refuge;
thou art all I have
in the land of the living.
Give me a hearing when I cry,
for I am brought very low.' *(Psalm 142.5-6)*

But my sorrow is deeper still, Father,
for I have to confess broken relationships,
lost friendships and so many people kept at arm's length.
And if that weren't all, there is the sorrow
that is born in the death of loved ones.
Life is cruel, Father,
so much to grieve for
in my failures,
in my pride,
in my loneliness.
I want to redeem my failures,
I want to be with those I have hurt,
I want to lose my self-pity,
I want to live again in your Spirit.

When my spirit is faint within me,
thou art there to watch over my steps.
'Set me free from my prison,
so that I may praise thy name.' *(Psalm 142.3,7)*

Teach me, my God and King,
In all things thee to see,
And what I do in anything
To do it as for thee.

A servant with this clause
Makes drudgery divine:
Who sweeps a room, as for thy laws,
Makes that and the action fine. *George Herbert*

Lord God, it is very hard to go through the routines of daily life and to accept them as opportunities for praising and serving you. The routines of personal hygiene, of waking and sleeping, of eating and drinking, do at least give us some personal satisfaction, and the daily round of family life cements our relationship with those near to us. But it is hard to see beyond the sameness of so many of our duties; so hard to overcome the fatigue and the boredom that attend some of life's essential chores — the washing up, cleaning the house, making the beds, the weekly washing, mowing the lawn, walking the dog . . .

Forgive us, Lord, for wanting everything to be exciting or different; for accepting the routines of others without gratitude, and for sometimes leaving the least interesting jobs for others to do.

We pray for those whose lives are filled with routines and who seldom experience something new:
unskilled workers on production lines,
labourers on the roads and in building,
typists who reproduce the work of others,
those who deliver milk, the mail and the newspapers,
workers on supermarket tills,
the unemployed,
severely handicapped people,
hospital patients, especially those in geriatric wards.

Lift us all above the duties and responsibilities of our daily lives so that we may see them in the light of your loving purposes and broaden our imaginations so that now and eternity may be seen as one moment in your time.

We give thee hearty thanks for the rest of the past night, and for the gift of a new day, with its opportunities of pleasing thee. Grant that we may so pass its hours in the freedom of thy service, that at eventide we may again give thanks unto thee; through Jesus Christ our Lord. Amen *(Eastern Church Liturgy)*

A new day lies open before me, Lord,
  a day with many duties and yet full of surprises.
I pause, before setting off on all that I have planned,
  to offer myself and this day into your hands.
Go with me through the day, unseen but not unknown,
  guiding me through difficulties, upholding me in danger,
  restraining me when I am straying from your paths.

Keep me faithful to the responsibilities that are mine,
  yet open to new possibilities of service.
Keep me firm against temptation,
  yet eager to enlarge my horizons.
Keep me fearless in the pursuit of truth,
  but always ready to forgive failure.

I pray that I may enter into all that today will bring
  with a desire to do your will, and yours alone.
When I meet strangers, make me welcoming,
  when I am offered advice, free me from prejudiced responses,
  when others meet with praise, save me from jealousy.

Sharpen my mind to receive new insights into life's meaning;
open my heart to respond in generosity to the needs of others;
renew in me a readiness to see your offer of yourself
  in those I have overlooked or shunned.
Surprise me, Lord, at each turn of the day,
  that even foreseen events take on new significance,
  and every moment glows with your glory.

'This day, Master, thou givest thy servant his discharge in peace;
now thy promise is fulfilled.
For I have seen with my own eyes
the deliverance which thou hast made ready in full view of all the nations:
a light that will be a revelation to the heathen,
and glory to thy people Israel.' *(Luke 2.29-32)*

Father, when you came to us in Jesus
you were a little child,
a homeless wanderer,
a religious teacher without status,
a washer of feet,
a crucified convict.
Yet many found new meaning in life through him:
Simeon was content to die,
John Baptist saw his prophecy come true,
Levi left the custom house,
Zacchaeus turned from extortion,
Saul became Paul,
and the Samaritan woman found her Saviour.

Father, so often we are seeking meaning
where it cannot be found:
in personal security,
in possessions and bank balances,
in public recognition,
in status and respectability.
Forgive us, Father, for not believing the gospel.
You have called us to a life of service;
you have promised us persecution and misunderstanding;
you have offered a cross.

Fulfil in us your calling to be your people
and receive us into the fellowship of your saints.

Finish then thy new creation,
Pure and spotless let us be;
Let us see thy great salvation,
Perfectly restored in thee;
Changed from glory into glory,
Till in heaven we take our place,
Till we cast our crowns before thee,
Lost in wonder, love, and praise. *Charles Wesley*

Today will bring its share of frustrations:
the petty annoyances like losing a key
or dropping a cup;
the big disappointments like failing a test
or breaking a limb.

Lord, life is full of set-backs
and I am not always able to cope.
I get angry or depressed,
full of self-pity or resentment.

I take it out on other people,
especially those who are closest to me
and who deserve my consideration.

Forgive me, Lord, for letting go of myself;
for wanting life to be smooth all the time;
for allowing adversity to cloud my vision
and upset my relationships.

Speak to me again of your never-failing goodness;
let me hear the affirmations that have sustained your people.

Read Psalm 121.

Dear Lord, I pray for those who carry heavy burdens,
who face the same difficulties day by day:
parents bringing up their children alone,
couples unhappily married,
young people without work,
those who have severe handicaps,
the families of prisoners,
elderly people unable to get out,
those known to me by name . . .
Let them know the comfort of the psalmist's conviction:

The Lord will guard you against all evil;
he will guard you, body and soul.
The Lord will guard your going and your coming,
now and for evermore. *(Psalm 121.7-8)*

From midday a darkness fell over the whole land, which lasted until three in the afternoon; and about three Jesus cried aloud, 'Eli, Eli, lema sabachthani?', which means, 'My God, my God, why hast thou forsaken me?' *(Matthew 27.45-46)*

Lord Jesus, you knew what it was to be alone;
to realise that no one else shared your vision
and that no one would stand with you;
to be deserted by all your friends;
even to doubt the presence of God.

If you could know such despair,
what chance of escape is there for us?
Stand with us in our times of need,
when we are afraid,
when we are full of grief,
when we have taken the wrong path,
and when we have hurt those we love most.
Stand with us that we may know that we are never alone.

Where can I escape from thy spirit?
Where can I flee from thy presence?
If I climb up to heaven, thou art there;
if I make my bed in Sheol, again I find thee.
If I take my flight to the frontiers of the morning
or dwell at the limit of the western sea,
even there thy hand will meet me
and thy right hand will hold me fast. *(Psalm 139.7-10)*

Lord Jesus, I pray for those who are lonely:
elderly people unable to get out,
disabled people entirely reliant on others,
those recently bereaved,
strangers in new areas,
long-term patients in psychiatric hospitals,
prisoners and their families,
those in positions of great responsibility,
pioneers of new ideas.
May they know the certainty of God's love and the security of his presence.

You must continue in your faith, firm on your foundations, never to be dislodged from the hope offered in the gospel. (Colossians 1.23)

Dear God, it is so hard to live with hope,
because so often our hopes have been confounded.

We long for a world of peace,
yet so many are killed and maimed in war.
We hope for a world of justice,
yet daily people starve to death,
and others are tortured for their beliefs.
We want the nations to work together,
and they go on stockpiling weapons.
These are the big hopes, Lord,
but when we turn to ourselves it is the same:
we hope for peace of mind,
and the unexpected brings confusion;
we long to be secure,
and we are beset by fears;
we strive for possessions,
but they do not satisfy.

Enlarge our hope, dear God,
till it is centred on him
who alone can fulfil it,
even Jesus Christ, our Saviour.

We pray for all who are without hope:
who trust in their own strength,
who live as if this world is all that matters,
who are so centred on themselves
that they cannot reach out to others in love.

Christ, our Saviour, come thou to dwell within us, that we may go forth with the light of thy hope in our eyes, and thy faith and love in our hearts. Amen (Gregorian Sacramentary)

The fear of the Lord is the beginning of wisdom,
and they who live by it grow in understanding.
(Psalm 111.10)

Father, it is not you I fear, for in Jesus you have shown yourself to be a God of love and mercy. In response to that love I try to live fearlessly, but I am human and the world is hostile to goodness.

I am afraid of the hostility and suspicion
caused by the world's divisions
between East and West, North and South.
I fear that the vision of One World
is fragile and there are few who pursue it.
I fear that my own community will break apart
and that many will be hurt in the conflict.
I fear that the different cultures will clash
rather than become the basis for joyful unity.

And there are more intimate fears, Lord.
I am afraid for my own safety in a world of violence,
for my own possessions in a world of greed.
I am afraid of the future. What will it bring?
Will my health continue?
Will I keep my job?
Will my family stay together?
Will my faith keep firm?

Father, forgive me for these fears,
for they work against your love
and they prevent me from living
in the joyful freedom of your Spirit.

There is no room for fear in love; perfect love banishes fear.
(1 John 4.18)

Banish my fears and increase my love, Lord,
but convince me again and again
that in your perfect love fear itself is destroyed,
and that such love is offered to me, fully and freely.

We know that if we only praise and commend virtue, this is not an adequate expression of the church's loyalty and is no way to help the government overcome present difficulties. Only by speaking the truth in love can we show positive concern for our nation's future.
(Presbyterian Church in Taiwan, 1975)

We are no longer to be children, tossed by the waves and whirled about by every fresh gust of teaching, dupes of crafty rogues and their deceitful schemes. No, let us speak the truth in love; so shall we fully grow up into Christ. *(Ephesians 4.14-15)*

Dear Lord, today as I go about my business,
I will be brought into conflict situations
    where one idea will vie with another;
    where one person's ambition
        will deny advance for someone else;
    where I will be presented with opposing claims
        and will be expected to make a judgement.

Forgive me, Lord, for being reluctant to speak,
    for having a false sense of duty,
    for being afraid of conflict.
Forgive me for misreading your gospel
    and for wanting to smooth over differences
        rather than confront them,
    for pursuing a false peace
        rather than a true reconciliation.

Let me not enter into conflict
for personal advantage or foolish pride,
but only for the sake of love.
Let love for your gospel and for all your people
be my sole motive for all that I do and say,
and when I am in the midst of conflict
take away from me all bitterness,
that I may speak the truth in love
and be open to the truth that others speak to me.

If rude reproach be o'er us flung,
And slander wound as with a sword,
Rule thou the unruly answering tongue,
And silence every vengeful word.

Whene'er in this wild world we meet
Unkindly deeds that anger move,
Teach us forgiveness, — triumph sweet,
To conquer evil will with love. *William Romanis*

I am a curious mixture, Lord.
I get so angry when my plans are thwarted;
and yet I can remain complacent
at the sufferings and trials of others.
I am not rational in my reactions,
otherwise I would be more consistent;
instead I flare up in resentment and rage,
and on a similar occasion I turn away unmoved.
Calm me down, Lord, when I am beginning to boil,
for so often I have hurt others in my anger.
I say words I do not really mean
and it is not easy afterwards to heal the wounds.
Yet, Lord, I pray that you will quicken my response
to the many injustices and hurts afflicting people,
especially when the powerful and the privileged
oppress the weak and the poor.
Anger is a strong emotion,
so often destructive in its results;
use my anger, Lord, only to fulfil your purpose.

A prayer for those whose anger has destroyed love
Father, I pray for all who have lived through the storm of spite and violence and have seen their hopes and their loves shattered. Keep alive, within them, the knowledge of forgiveness and the spirit of reconciliation that they may continue to reflect your goodness and may go on to heal the broken relationships.

Nature **Day 19**

To see a World in a Grain of Sand
And a Heaven in a Wild Flower. *William Blake*

The heavens tell out the glory of God,
the vault of heaven reveals his handiwork.
(Psalm 19.1)

Heavenly Father, Creator and Sustainer of the universe,
before the works of your hands I am struck dumb with wonder.
Again and again you surprise me with the beauty of the earth.
I look up and the sky is new every morning;
day by day the face of nature changes.
I stumble upon the tiny flower and am startled by its colours;
I watch the spider weave its web and can scarcely believe what I see;
the relentless movement of the sea echoes the beating of my heart;
the bird's cry as the cat pounces disturbs my peace of mind.

Father, I cannot express what I feel about the world you have made.
Delight and fear, awe and curiosity:
so many emotions mingle together.

Forgive me for taking so much for granted,
and for not caring enough for all that you have given.

Father, I pray for all who work closely with nature:
for farmers and gardeners who grow our food,
for scientists and technicians who probe the secrets of the earth,
for foresters who plant and harvest the trees,
for those who forecast the weather,
for photographers and artists who capture the beauty for others to see,
for conservationists and all who guard the precious heritage of the earth.

Read Genesis 1.1 to 2.4, the poetic account of the creation of the world with its refrain, 'and God saw that it was good'.
Give thanks to God for his good creation.

Thine still the changeful beauty of the hills,
The purple valleys flecked with silver rills,
The ocean glistening 'neath the golden rays;
They all are thine, and voiceless speak thy praise.

Thou dost the strength to workman's arm impart;
From thee the skilled musician's mystic art,
The grace of poet's pen or painter's hand,
To teach the loveliness of sea and land.

Ernest Edward Dugmore

O God, Creator of so much startling beauty,
I praise you for the work of painters and sculptors
adding to the pleasure of life
under the spell of your handiwork.
Through their imagination and skill
we are made aware of the splendour of the earth
as well as the poignancy of human experience.
They expose us to truth as they see it,
enhancing our appreciation of line and form,
vividly experimenting with colour and texture,
showing us how glorious and precious is your world.
I give thanks for the great artists
whose work endures till today:
those who built the great cathedrals of medieval Europe
and stocked them with such lavish decoration;
those who recorded the customs and great events of history
in paintings, tapestries and friezes;
those who gave visual form to the stories of the Bible
in murals, on ceilings and in stained glass;
those who captured a moment of rapture
and fixed it for others to enjoy.

I pray for all who live by art
and all who teach others how to paint and draw and sculpt.
Bless their work that it may bring pleasure to others.
Develop in me an appreciation of all that is lovely.

O praise the Lord.
O praise God in his holy place,
praise him in the vault of heaven, the vault of his power;
praise him for his mighty works,
praise him for his immeasurable greatness.
Praise him with fanfares on the trumpet,
praise him upon lute and harp;
praise him with tambourines and dancing,
praise him with flute and strings;
praise him with the clash of cymbals,
praise him with triumphant cymbals;
let everything that has breath praise the Lord!
O praise the Lord. *(Psalm 150)*

Music is a special delight, Lord,
soothing me when I am troubled,
moving me to tears by its intensity,
thrilling me by its pace and richness.

I give thanks for the music of the seasons,
in bird song and insect drone,
in wind and flowing water,
in the rustle of leaves,
and in the crash of thunder.

I give thanks for the work of composers
making music of all kinds to bring pleasure;
and for all who perform as soloists,
members of choirs and orchestras,
dance bands and small groups.

I give thanks for the different musical styles
appealing to a variety of moods:
for popular music with its rhythms,
and orchestral music full in tone;
for the music of dance and marching,
and folk songs and choirs;
for musical accompaniment
in theatre, film and concert hall.

Father, I thank you for the music of worship and devotion for through our hymns and psalms and spiritual songs we are able to express our faith and lift up our hearts in praise and gratitude to your glorious Name. Amen

A good book is the precious life-blood of a master spirit, embalmed and treasured up on purpose to a life beyond life. (John Milton)

Lord I have grown so much through the writings of others:
I have learnt facts and considered opinions,
I have seen aspects of human nature
which I have not experienced at first hand,
I have been carried away in imagination
through the craft of the story-teller,
my prejudices and attitudes have been challenged
and sometimes they have been changed.

Lord, I thank you for so much literature:
for newspapers and magazines,
for reference and text books,
for novels, poetry and biography,
for books of prayer and devotion,
and above all for the Bible.

Every inspired scripture has its use for teaching the truth and refuting error, or for reformation of manners and discipline in right living, so that the man who belongs to God may be efficient and equipped for good work of every kind. (2 Timothy 3.16-17)

Lord, I pray for the work of the Bible Societies in printing and distributing the scriptures, for those who translate them into the languages of the modern world, and for those who interpret them so that your word may be heard and believed. Bless the work of all who write that they may quicken the imagination and bear witness to the truth, that all who read may be inspired by your Holy Spirit to turn to you in love, for Christ's sake. Amen

'Do not store up for yourselves treasure on earth, where it grows rusty and moth-eaten, and thieves break in to steal it. Store up treasure in heaven, where there is no moth and no rust to spoil it, no thieves to break in and steal. For where your treasure is, there will your heart be also.' *(Matthew 6.19-20)*

Jesus said to his disciples, 'I tell you this: a rich man will find it hard to enter the kingdom of Heaven. I repeat, it is easier for a camel to pass through the eye of a needle than for a rich man to enter the kingdom of God.' *(Matthew 19.23-24)*

Lord, we want to react as the disciples did,
'Then who can be saved?'
We do not fully understand your answer
that everything is possible for God,
for the rebuke is still there,
the doubt about our faithfulness
is even more acute in this affluent society.
What are we to do? Should we opt out?
Should we renounce our possessions?
We sing the hymn confessing
we are rich in things and poor in soul,
but we do not know how to escape.
Forgive us for our overdependence on things
and our lack of trust in loving relationships.
Forgive us for being rich in a poor world;
for using so many of the earth's resources
when there are poor and hungry people
whose silent cries beat on our deaf ears.
Forgive us for misusing your gifts
and for taking too many of them.

Lord, release us from shame and guilt, that we may joyfully share the good things of the earth, regarding all our possessions as a trust from you to be used for your glory.

Then he took a cup, and after giving thanks he said, 'Take this and share it among yourselves; for I tell you, from this moment I shall drink from the fruit of the vine no more until the time when the kingdom of God comes.' And he took bread, gave thanks, and broke it; and he gave it to them, with the words: 'This is my body.'
(Luke 22.17-19)

Father, it is one of the mysteries of Christianity
that Jesus took the ordinary provisions of life
and offered them as channels of your grace.
We praise you for the ordinary meals,
when in fellowship with one another
we find sustenance for body and spirit.
We praise you for the variety of provisions
stocking our larders and tempting our appetites;
for the basic nourishment of bread and water,
and for the fruits and vegetables,
the proteins and the vitamins,
making our meals varied and exciting.
We praise you for those special meals
when we break bread and pour the cup
to remember our Lord and to share his life.
We praise you for making yourself known to us
and for receiving us as we are.
Go on giving us, Father, food and drink
for life in this world and for eternal life.

Father, we pray for those who do not have enough to eat and drink: some elderly people who are too frail to care for themselves; children who are neglected by their parents; the poor in so many countries; refugees and those caught up in famine and war. They are your people, too, Father, and we offer ourselves to work while it is still day so that at evening they may sit with us to enjoy the fruits of the earth. Show us how that offer may be turned into the food and drink by which they may live, for Christ's sake. Amen

Politics **Day 25**

The authorities are in God's service. *(Romans 13.6)*

Father, I am bewildered by the newspaper stories;
I find it hard to interpret what I see on the news.
World history is being made every day
and I cannot read the signs of the times.
Politicians appeal for my support;
they speak with firmness and authority
but I do not know what to think;
I am not sure where truth lies.

Lord, save me from easy acceptance of persuasive arguments,
yet save me from not caring about world events.
Forgive me for not protesting against injustice
and for being so captured by my own comfort.
Forgive me for not working enough for peace
and for being content with my own security.
Forgive me for allowing others to speak out
while I remain complacent and quiet.

Pray for the local councillors in your area, for your Member of Parliament, for the members of the Government, and all world leaders.

Lord, inspire the politicians to choose right priorities,
to have special concern for the poor and the weak,
to put an end to oppression and injustice,
and to work for peace and human development.
Give those who have power the humility and courage
to use it in the service of all people.
Give me the will and the wisdom
to share in making the world more like your kingdom.

Almighty Father, who by thy Son Jesus Christ hast sanctified labour to the welfare of mankind: prosper, we pray thee, the industries of this land and all those who are engaged therein; that, shielded in all their temptations and dangers, and receiving a due reward of their labours, they may praise thee by living according to thy will; through Jesus Christ our Lord. Amen (*Prayer Book as proposed in 1928*)

Our lives are surrounded by the products of industry;
we live comfortably because of all that is manufactured;
the modern world is shaped by industrial enterprise;
millions of people find life's meaning through their work.

God, Creator and Sustainer of life, we praise you
for industrial output in the service of mankind,
for inventiveness and efficiency,
for good relations between management and workers,
for the creation of wealth and its fair distribution.
We ask forgiveness for our share
in the greed which industry has encouraged,
in the military power which it has fed,
in the widening gap between haves and have-nots,
in the misuse of the earth's resources.

Father, the news brings us face to face with the conflicts and misunderstandings that begin in the breakdown of communications between employers and employees, but threaten the health and the stability of whole communities. Give all who are involved an understanding of the limitations of human imagination and charity towards those who hold different opinions. Save us all from prejudiced positions and, when we are involved in conflict, keep us searching for new initiatives to break deadlock and achieve agreement.

Pray for those industries that are in the news today . . .
because of new contracts,
because of new products or models,
because of industrial unrest,
because of redundancies and closures.

They shall beat their swords into mattocks
and their spears into pruning-knives;
nation shall not lift sword against nation
nor ever again be trained for war,
and each man shall dwell under his own vine,
under his own fig-tree, undisturbed.
For the Lord of Hosts himself has spoken. *(Micah 4.3-4)*

God, our Father, I long for a peaceful world,
where children may grow up without fear,
and the old may die quietly and serenely.
I long for a world where security is built on trust
and not threat;
where science is devoted to the production of food
and not the development of weapons;
where nations work together against poverty and disease
and not against each other.

I pray for the United Nations, and all its specialised Agencies, in its work for peace. Prosper all that it does in peace-keeping, in its emphasis on human rights, in its programmes of health care and nutrition, and in its relief work among the poor and refugees. Bless all who work for it and keep them faithful to the vision of a world in which disputes may be settled round a table and not in armed conflict.

Prayer for Peace
Lead me from death to life, from falsehood to truth;
Lead me from despair to hope, from fear to trust;
Lead me from hate to love, from war to peace;
Let peace fill our heart, our world, our universe.

Jesus said: Happy are those who work for peace;
God will call them his children! *(Matthew 5.9, GNB)*

My object all sublime
I shall achieve in time —
To let the punishment fit the crime. — *W.S. Gilbert*

Father God, when I read the daily papers,
with the news of so much crime,
of people maimed and killed,
of property stolen and desecrated,
I am tempted to curse the criminals
and to want their punishment to fit their crimes.

Read the story of Cain and Abel from Genesis 4.1-16.

Father, the crimes of humanity
are an affront to your image in which we are made.
Instil in us all a reverence for life
and a respect for the possessions of others.
When we are tempted to do wrong,
restrain us.
When we meet the victims of crime,
give us compassion.
When we judge the conduct of others,
fill us with your mercy.
When we condemn others,
forgive us.

Father, I pray for those who are in prison:
those who are convicted for crime,
those who are awaiting trial,
those who have committed no crime.

I pray too for the families of prisoners, that they may find community and support; for those who administer justice, that they may temper firmness with mercy; for those who serve in the prisons, that they may create communities of hope and purpose.

'This may be the child who will make the difference in our future.' These words were spoken by a nurse in reply to an onlooker at a childbirth who wondered: 'Wouldn't it be better if this baby died right now instead of having to live in poverty?'

God, our Father, forgive us that children are born into poverty while we enjoy the riches of your creation. Forgive us for our complacency in the face of such deprivation and for our unwillingness to change the world into a place of plenty for all. Forgive us for not protesting against the neglect and despair which so many experience.

Father of all people, we pray for the poor:
homeless people seeking shelter,
unemployed people wanting work,
hungry people foraging for food,
mothers crying for their children,
refugees fleeing in fear.
We know that their poverty is a rebuke to us all,
for they are at the bottom of the world's priorities,
they cannot make decisions about their future,
they are victims of other people's greed and neglect.
Awaken us to a sense of outrage and a spirit of compassion;
show us how to engage in the struggle of the poor
for an end to injustice,
for a new world, one world,
in which all your people
will have the basic needs
for a full and fulfilling life.

Read the parable of the talents in Matthew 25.14-30.

Lord God, we are all created in your image
and in Jesus Christ you call us to share your glory.
We praise you for all that you have given to people:
the ability to reason and to plan,
manual skills and artistic talents,
the capacity to dream and to imagine,
the courage of endurance and the power of love.
Lord, in all these gifts we glimpse your boundless energy
drawing out the creative urge you planted within us.

Today a few will make headlines with their achievements:
the successful film,
the scientific breakthrough,
the clever invention,
the broken record,
the spectacular business deal,
the political triumph.
Lord, bless all that contributes to human welfare
and all that is part of your loving purpose.

There will be many more achievements that will go unnoticed except
by those who are most closely affected:
the first steps of the child, the first faltering words,
the courageous effort after serious illness,
the reconciliation after quarrel and bitterness,
the first day at work,
and the daily task faithfully completed.
Lord, bless all who use your good gifts well,
forgive us when we fail or offer second best,
renew your Spirit within us and use our achievements
to the honour and glory of your Holy Name.

Sport

When I think of all the sporting activity
in my own area, nationally and world-wide,
I am amazed, Lord, to what lengths people will go
to break records, to beat opponents, to show their skill.
I praise you for the poise and rhythm of the body,
for its strength and its endurance,
for the co-ordination of hand and eye
making possible such graceful and swift movements.

But I am sad when I realise how sportsmen are used to prove national
and racial superiority.
Lord, forgive us for the tribalism of so much sport:
for the violence and self-seeking,
for the greed and the corruption
which so often surround it.

I pray, Lord, for all engaged in sporting activity:
in the big events that catch the headlines,
and in the numerous matches and contests
in my own area, in schools, and clubs,
and among families and friends.
Let pleasure and healthy exercise be the motive,
and let the enjoyment and friendly rivalry
contribute to the building up of community life.

Entertainment

I pray for all who entertain, Lord,
in local amateur performances,
in the recognised centres of cultural life,
in films and on radio and television.
Make them conscious of their influence
and its potential for good or evil.
Give them a sense of proportion
and a desire to seek the highest standards of their art.
Set their minds on all that is true,
all that is noble,
all that is just and pure,
all that is lovable and gracious,
whatever is excellent and admirable.
Fill their thoughts and hearts
with these things and your love will prevail.

THE WAY OF LIFE

LIFE IN GOD

The God of love **Day 1**

Everyone who loves is a child of God and knows God, but the unloving know nothing of God. For God is love; and his love was disclosed to us in this, that he sent his only Son into the world to bring us life. *(1 John 4.8-9)*

Father, you are love . . .
though I blunder in the ways of my loving,
as child, friend, spouse, parent,
stumbling over my selfishness, weighed down by my failures,
you do not change and your love does not end.

Father, you are love . . .
when love eludes us, you come to find us;
when love causes us pain, you come to heal us;
when love calls us to sacrifice, you grant us strength;
when love grows cold, you come as fire to warm us into life again.

Father, you are love . . .
the prize we seek above all others:
you are that for which we long more than anything;
in you, we know that we are truly loved,
from you, we learn how truly to love.

An act of praise and thanksgiving
Father, with all things that, in your love, you have created, I lift my heart in praise to you. Your love draws us to you, deep calling to deep. It is our home, that from which we came and to which we shall return.

Father, thank you
for those whose love shows me something of your love,
for the joy I find in loving others,
for love's endurance beyond all things.

A prayer for others
Father, we pray that you will forgive and renew all those who have failed in their loving. May they reaffirm the promises they have broken. May they shut the door on all the bitter memories of the past and look with trust and hope to the future. For Jesus' sake.

Holy, holy, holy, Lord God almighty!
Early in the morning our song shall rise to thee;
Holy, holy, holy, merciful and mighty,
God in three Persons, blessed Trinity! Reginald Heber

God is the Other who, in his love, calls us to become what his good will desires we should be and gives us strength to respond to his call.

Lord, Holy Father, God in mystery and in majesty,
we worship you,
with the angels who hide their faces,
we adore you,
with the glorious assembly of your people in heaven,
we shout our alleluias,
with all our brothers and sisters on earth,
we exult in your love.

Lord God, you are not the work of our hands,
a talisman to protect us from evil,
a mysterious spiritual force to which we can dictate our wishes,
a projection of our childish fantasies.
You are the one, the holy, the living God,
Other than we are, beyond even our highest imaginings.

Lord God, we are the work of your hands;
in freedom you call us to share with you in the joy of your creation,
in love, you strengthen us that we might do your will:
the demand and the succour – you grant us both,
what you ask of us, that you also give.

Help us, Father, to make real your goodness in our lives. May the vision of your glory be our inspiration in our daily living, that what is ordinary and commonplace may be touched with the fire of heaven.

Let justice roll on like a river
and righteousness like an ever-flowing stream. *(Amos 5.24)*

Father, you are a God of justice and compassion.
Your compassion drives you into the world to seek justice for the poor, the hungry, the oppressed, the victims of cruelty, the vulnerable and the unprotected.
You do not come amongst us blind-folded,
impartially holding at arms' length the scales of justice:
you come as fierce love,
standing at the side of those whose cause you plead and whose deliverance you seek.

Forgive us, Father,
when we are deaf to the cries that ring in your ears,
blind to the misery that you see,
inactive in an unjust world you seek to change,
helpless against the evil that you have conquered.

Father, may our prayers never be a form of escape or our worship a shutting out of the world:
to behold you in prayer and to praise you in worship is to stand face to face with a justice that seeks the liberty and well-being of every man and woman.
May our praying be a true sharing of your burden and our worship a sacrifice of love offered on behalf of the whole world.

A prayer for those who suffer injustice
Lord, be with those who day by day bear the brunt of the world's inhumanity. Bring nearer the day of their deliverance. May they never lose their trust in the final justice that rules all things.
Lord, we pray for those who persecute and oppress their fellow beings. Lead them to repentance that they may be forgiven.

O Lord our God, arise;
The cause of truth maintain,
And wide o'er all the peopled world
Extend her blessed reign. *Ralph Wardlaw*

Father, we acknowledge your truth:
we praise you, for with you there are no lies,
no deception,
no half-truths;
your truth does not change with changing circumstances;
always you are the same.

Show us the truth, Father, and help us to believe it and to accept it:
may the word of scripture guide our consciences and shape our actions so that what we think and what we do may be honest and not cause us shame;
may the Holy Spirit enlighten our minds that we may understand the word of Christ and build our lives upon his truth.

Jesus said, 'You shall know the truth, and the truth will set you free.' (John 8.32)

Let us pray for others . . .
For those who work in television and newspapers,
that they may be servants of the truth;
for those whose word is trusted – teachers, police, doctors, preachers,
that they may not betray their trust;
for those who govern,
that they may not twist the truth in order to oppress and tyrannise;
for writers, artists, film-makers and poets,
that they may share a vision of the truth with all of us.

The angels keep their ancient places; —
Turn but a stone and start a wing!
'Tis ye, 'tis your estrangèd faces,
That miss the many-splendoured thing.

Francis Thompson

Praise the Lord out of heaven;
  praise him in the heights.
Praise him, all his angels;
  praise him, all his host.
Praise him, sun and moon;
  praise him, all you shining stars;
praise him, heaven of heavens,
  and you waters above the heavens.

(Psalm 148.1-4)

Father, the world fills our senses,
  it ravishes our sight,
  we savour it in our nostrils,
  it crowds into our ears,
  it is alive to our touch.
May we not despise what is material as if it were a distraction
    from what is unseen and eternal.
In joy you made the world:
  may we enjoy it as you do.
May we look, and breathe, and listen, and touch
  with faith and sensitivity,
    that in the glory of what you have made
    we may behold the glory of what you are.

Praying for others

Pray for people who are responsible for the preservation of the earth:
  those who study the balance of nature and how it may be maintained;
  those who protect endangered species in the animal kingdom . . .
Pray for those who are responsible for the earth's resources:
  those who harvest and distribute the sources of energy;
  those who farm the earth and grow our food . . .

A thanksgiving

Father, for all that you have made, accept my gratitude. May I show that gratitude in the way I use all the material things you give me.

Jesus said, 'I have come that men may have life, and may have it in all its fullness.' *(John 10.10)*

Lord, when we look for happiness it eludes us,
it seems like Atlantis,
a lost world never to be discovered.
It is happiness that finds us,
taking us by surprise,
hidden in those things that we sought
because they were good in themselves,
because we loved them;
happiness was the reward for our seeking, not its end and object.

Lord, it is to you we come in our times of need:
when we are sick and need healing,
when we are lost and need guidance,
when we feel inadequate and need your strength,
when we are uncertain and ask for reassurance.
At times like this we expect to find you.
Why do we not have the same expectations of our happiness?

Lord, make us more aware of your presence in all that delights us:
in the laughter of friends,
in the sense of fulfilment that we find in our work,
in the touch of someone we love,
in the exhilaration of physical exercise,
in the beginning of each new day.
You have given us life,
this place, this moment:
grant us happiness in accepting what we are and where we are.

Father, we pray for those who are distrustful of happiness, because it has been snatched away from them in the past. We pray for those who, by nature, are pessimistic or melancholy and, seeing only the shadows, fail to see the light by which they are cast. May your presence help them to accept life's happiness without fear or mistrust.

Suffering can face us with the most daunting challenge to what we believe. It can also bring us into a deeper relationship with God than we had known before.

Pray
for those known to you, people whom you love,
friends, acquaintances, who are suffering;
for the people you read about in the newspaper,
or hear about on radio or television,
who, in various parts of the world, are suffering;
for people whose suffering is not obvious to others,
those whose minds are tortured by bitter memories or anxieties,
those whose relationships have turned sour,
bringing pain and regret,
those who are lonely, or frightened, or full of despair;
for those who care for the suffering,
that their compassion, patience and understanding may be constantly renewed.

Father, help us to overcome the fears that rise up within us when we are faced with suffering. Give us courage, hope and cheerfulness, that these may aid our healing. May the experience of suffering draw us into a deeper knowledge of you as, with faith, we trust ourselves to your healing love. Be with us as we share the suffering of those we love. We cannot take their pain into our bodies, but in their weakness may they know our strength, may they feel our prayers like a rock beneath them, and may the touch of our hand be a signal of love.

A thanksgiving
Father, I give you thanks for all those times when you have been with me in moments of weakness and suffering. More than ever before, your love seemed all about me and beneath me. I remember with gratitude the encouragement of friends and the care of those who were closest to me. May the remembrance of your goodness fill all the coming days with confidence and with hope.

St Paul wrote: 'I have learned to find resources in myself whatever my circumstances. I know what it is to be brought low, and I know what it is to have plenty. I have been very thoroughly initiated into the human lot with all its ups and downs — fullness and hunger, plenty and want. I have strength for anything through him who gives me power.' *(Philippians 4.12-13)*

Lord Jesus Christ, you promised us that adversity is to be expected in this life,
you told us that following you means carrying a cross;
the blessed in your Kingdom are the vulnerable:
those who mourn, those who weep, those who stand between the hostility of others.

Yet adversity still takes us by surprise:
the gathering clouds dismay us;
we pray for love, joy and peace, and are resentful when a cross seems the only answer to our prayers;
and there are times when the Kingdom seems to ask too much of us.
Why do we have to mourn before we are comforted?
Why weep before we can laugh?
Why can't we be left to get on with our own lives and not be drawn into other people's hatreds, wars, arguments, bitterness?

Lord, give us the grace to accept everything as an opportunity of growing closer to you:
may we know that we need the hardening of frost, the streaming rain, as well as the comfortable sun, if we are to grow to maturity; may every cross that we carry be itself a sign of resurrection, and may the blessedness of the Kingdom be ours in those experiences that we find hard to accept.

For others
Pray for all whom you know who pass through difficult times; that they may know the power of Christ and the commitment of our love for them.

God's commitment to us

Day 9

This is where everything begins — with God's commitment to us. If we put it the other way around and make everything depend upon our commitment to God, then faith will go beyond our reach.

Jesus said, 'Be assured, I am with you always, to the end of time.'
(Matthew 28.20)

God be praised!
As sure as night and day,
as real as the ground beneath our feet,
as certain as yesterday,
so is the Lord's love to us.

There is no greater commitment than
the taking of human flesh,
a death upon a cross,
a resurrection,
and all this God has done for us in Jesus,
plunging into the very depths of hell itself
to bring us to the joys of Paradise.

Lord God, you let nothing stand in the way of your love:
you break down the barrier of our sin with your forgiveness,
when we stumble in failure you lift us up,
our pride, our stubbornness, our naive conviction that we always
know what is best for ourselves, you bear with infinite patience,
there is nowhere that you would not come to us,
there will never be a time when your love will end.

For reflection
As I have given thanks for God's commitment to me,
I think of my commitment to others:
the people I love,
the people to whom I have made promises,
the people with whom I share my life in the church.
Lord, as you are faithful, so keep me faithful.

'All will hate you for your allegiance to me; but the man who holds out to the end will be saved.' *(Matthew 10.22)*

Father, our God,
save us from all those things that would threaten our commitment to you,
save us from all that makes for triviality.
We worship you in your love, your holiness, your justice and your truth;
may our understanding of you never be less than that;
may faith not become an optional extra in life,
a crutch to lean on when everything else has failed,
a passing interest fitted into a busy schedule.

We ask, Father,
that our hearts may be constantly renewed by the fire of your love,
that our vision of your glory may not diminish with the years,
that faith may always be a glorious enterprise,
a consuming passion, a matter of life and death,
a burning conviction;
may you be the centre of our whole being.

John Wesley's Covenant Prayer
I am no longer my own, but yours. Put me to what you will, rank me with whom you will; put me to doing, put me to suffering; let me be employed for you or laid aside for you, exalted for you or brought low for you; let me be full, let me be empty; let me have all things, let me have nothing; I freely and wholeheartedly yield all things to your pleasure and disposal. And now, glorious and blessed God, Father, Son, and Holy Spirit, you are mine and I am yours. So be it. And the covenant made on earth, let it be ratified in heaven. Amen

The Covenant Community **Day 11**

Christians, wherever they are, do not live the life of faith in isolation. To belong to Jesus is to belong to the great and mystical community of his church.

Blest be the tie that binds
Our hearts in Christian love;
The fellowship of kindred minds
Is like to that above.
John Fawcett

Lord God, you have made your covenant with us in Jesus, your Son:
you have committed yourself to us, in love, for all eternity,
you have called us to be faithful unto death;
you are pledged to us,
we are pledged to you.

Father, in calling us to covenant with you,
you have not called us to a partnership of equals:
yours is always the initiative,
you first loved us,
your promises are not conditional upon ours,
it is your grace that favours us,
not our faith that bestows something on you.

Sometimes, Lord, we are tempted to think of ourselves as chosen for our virtue, or our worthiness, or because we are decent, law-abiding people:
as if being in covenant with you meant nothing more than maintaining ordinary, Western, middle-class values;
faith, we think, is your approval of our life-style, your reassurance that somehow, by muddling along as best we can, we shall find ourselves on 'the right road'.

Father, your covenant with us was made in the suffering of Calvary:
may we accept the cost of being called,
may the way of covenant be the way of the cross.

If we are to speak of what is divine and unseen, we must use earthly language. We have to take truths that are part of our daily experience and rummage through our vocabulary to find the right words. Then the experience becomes a picture of God's love for us and our words a feeble attempt to describe it. So we think of the Church as the Bride of Christ, seeing in the loving, faithful relationship of man and wife a picture of Christ's love for his people.

An act of praise
Lord Jesus Christ, you have come in love to us:
you came to win us to yourself and make us your own forever;
you came that you might share your life with us and we share our lives with you.
Lord, with all your people,
in every generation and every part of the world,
we praise you for the love that has made us your own.

A thanksgiving
Lord, our human love is an image of your divine love:
we thank you for every way in which we see love in others,
the love of man and wife,
of parent and child;
love between friends,
the love that binds us together as Christians.
May we never accept ungratefully the love that is offered to us,
but value it as a gift without price.

Praying for others
Pray for your own family and the families of your friends,
that your love and their love may reflect Christ's love for all of us.
Pray especially for families where love is breaking down
between man and wife
or between children and parents.

I kneel in prayer to the Father, from whom every family in heaven and on earth takes its name, that out of the treasures of his glory he may grant you strength and power through his Spirit in your inner being, that through faith Christ may dwell in your hearts in love.
(Ephesians 3.14-16)

Father, we thank you for our life together in the family of your church:
for the people you give to us to share together our life in Christ;
for the gifts shared amongst us, different gifts for different people, which together build the church in health, vigour and unity;
for the privilege of sharing one another's lives:
the shared joy and love,
the encouraging touch of sympathy,
the common bond of truth believed and proclaimed.

Father, bless the family of the church. May we accept one another as brothers and sisters, finding strength and joy in our life together. May we be a family open to all the families of mankind that, in the church, they may overcome all the hostilities and prejudices that might otherwise drive them apart.

Father, we pray for all families:
may they not build castle walls of mistrust about themselves,
nor may the love and loyalty they have for one another keep them from being loving and loyal to those outside the family;
may they learn to handle conflict and not freeze their anger in distant politeness nor tear themselves apart in verbal hatred.

Say the family prayer: 'Our father . . .'.

You are a chosen race, a royal priesthood, a dedicated nation, and a people claimed by God for his own. *(1 Peter 2.9)*

A priest is someone who stands before people as the representative of God, and before God as the representative of people.

Lord God, you have placed in our hands the gift that you want us to share with everyone: the Good News of Jesus Christ.
You offer forgiveness to all in their sin,
in their brokenness, in their alienation,
in their failure and in their guilt.
You offer the way of life to those who grope in darkness,
experimenting with every new religious heresy,
sampling every craze and every novelty,
yet finding no direction, no purpose.
You offer eternal life to all of us,
trapped between our birth and our death,
racing against time.
You give yourself,
the Father of us all,
desiring the greatest good for each one of us,
pursuing us in your love.

Lord, Father, this is what you give to your church, and this is what you intend for all mankind:
make us faithful in offering to others what you have given us;
may we not give stones instead of bread.

Father, accept what we offer on behalf of others,
accept our prayers for those who do not know how to pray for themselves,
accept our faith and our belief on behalf of those who cannot find faith and who find it hard to believe,
accept our suffering on behalf of others, whenever we are called to suffer:
as we pray for the family of mankind,
Lord, in your mercy hear our prayer.

Jesus said, 'In very truth I tell you, a servant is not greater than his master, nor a messenger than the one who sent him.' (John 13.16)

An act of thanksgiving

Lord Jesus Christ, we thank you for showing us what it means to be a servant:

you have shown us that in serving others we do not demean ourselves;

in service we are one with you and share your work.

For setting us free from all status-seeking and from envy,

we thank you, Lord.

Praying for ourselves and others

Lord God, we pray for one another in the service to which you have called each one of us:

for those called to the responsibility of leadership,

that their vocation may not be burdened with loneliness but shared in the companionship of all their brothers and sisters in Christ;

for those who do the thankless tasks of the Kingdom:

serving people who have opted out of society into vagrancy, or drugs, or abuse of alcohol;

working with the violent young, the vandaliser, the bitter and the unresponsive;

for those who work with the aged,

endeavouring to bring dignity and compassion to those whose physical and mental powers are failing;

and for all your people we pray:

may we see that each of us is called to a way of service,

may the place of our daily work be the place where we seek your glory,

may we not grow crabby, self-important, tired or resentful in your service:

teach us to use our resources wisely,

renew us day by day.

Lord, thy word abideth,
And our footsteps guideth;
Who its truth believeth
Light and joy receiveth. H.W. Baker

Lord God, we bless you for all those events that lie behind the holy scriptures:

for your revelation of yourself in the history of your people, Israel,
for the prophets who discerned your purpose and heard your voice,
for the coming of him who was promised through the ages, Jesus Christ,
for his word of truth,
for his life in our midst,
for his death upon the cross,
for his resurrection on the third day,
for the coming of the Holy Spirit,
and for the birth of the Church.

Lord, we bless you for those who faithfully recorded and interpreted the things that they heard and saw:

for their word, through which we hear your word to us,
for their testimony to Christ, through which Christ is given to us now,
for their record of the acts of the Holy Spirit, which enables us to experience his power and presence now.

Lord, bless your people as they listen to the scriptures today.

May the truth inspire our actions and keep guard of our conscience,
may the Church be constantly renewed and reformed by its encounter with the word;
help us as we strive to explain its meaning to others, that they, with us, may find eternal life.

This is the day that the Lord has made; we shall rejoice and be glad in it.

In our daily lives . . .

Father, the world is alive with your presence:
worship and adoration rise up unbidden within me
as yet again the world takes me by surprise.
I hear your voice in
a note of music,
a familiar voice,
the sound of the sea.
I see you near
in the rising sun,
in the unchanging mountains,
in a wild flower.
Father, accept the praise of such holy moments.

In the fellowship of the church . . .

Father, we rejoice that you have given us Sunday:
the day when we remember that you created the world and all that is within it,
the day when Jesus was raised from the dead, and death and hell laid waste,
the day in which all things were made and re-made.

Father, may we approach Sunday with longing and expectation;
as the hungry seek for bread,
so may we yearn for word and sacrament;
save our worship from all that is trivial;
rooted in the reality of the world in which we live,
may it yet glimpse the glory of your presence,
and stand in awe at the light of your holiness;
may we sense the presence of all who have gone before us,
hearing in our own songs the echo of unseen heaven's praise.

From earth to heaven we build a stair,
The name by which we call it, prayer.
Narayan Vaman Tilak

Father, we sometimes lose sight of prayer,
we treat it as a last resort,
something to fall back on when everything else has failed;
we let it become the first casualty of our too-busy lives,
crowded out by our overloaded schedules;
we give up praying,
because it is difficult,
because our prayers don't seem to be answered,
because we run out of words,
because we can't handle silence.

Lord Jesus, the disciples found prayer difficult as well:
it didn't come any more naturally to them
than it does to us,
so we ask you, as they asked you . . .
Lord, teach us how to pray.
When words fail us, may we know the power of silence and so learn to listen before we talk;
teach us how to identify with others in their need, that our caring may be a part of our praying.

Lord, help us to pray together in ways that are honest and full of faith:
may we not generalise when we know of particular needs;
give us a brave heart that we may be specific in the things for which we pray, knowing that you answer in many ways and that one day we shall understand what now mystifies us;
we ask also that we may not limit our prayers solely to those whom we know by name; give us faith to pray for distant needs, for the massive international problems of the human family, and the countless multitudes whose cry ascends to heaven.

When we bless 'the cup of blessing', is it not a means of sharing in the blood of Christ? When we break the bread, is it not a means of sharing in the body of Christ? Because there is one loaf, we, many as we are, are one body; for it is one loaf of which we all partake.
(1 Corinthians 10.16-17)

A thanksgiving

Lord, I thank you for all that I have shared with my brothers and sisters in Christ at your holy table.
It has been holy ground,
a place of awesome remembrance,
a blessed eucharist, feast of thanksgiving.
Lord, I thank you for our eating and drinking together,
for the bread from the soil that our brothers have tilled,
for the wine from the vine that they have tended:
these earthly things, through the touch of your Spirit,
have made it possible for us to share in Christ, again and again.

A prayer at communion

Lord, may this be a place of joy,
for Christ is in the midst of us;
as our memories are quickened,
we recall the promises you have made to us
and we have made to you.
May the memory stir up faith and obedience in us;
let us rejoice in Christ risen from the dead,
filling this moment with glory,
made known to us in the breaking of bread.

Lord, may we renew our covenant with one another around this holy table:
this bread, broken and shared amongst us,
unites us and makes us one,
this wine, the sign of sacrifice,
renews the joy of our salvation
and calls us to be the servant people of God.

It was there from the beginning; we have heard it; we have seen it with our own eyes; we looked upon it, and felt it with our own hands; and it is of this we tell. Our theme is the word of life.

(1 John 1.1)

Father, thank you for the truth,
thank you for all who have lived by the truth,
thank you for all who have died for the truth,
thank you for all who make the truth clearer to us,
thank you for your Spirit who helps us to understand and obey the truth.

Lord God, you have uttered your word of truth,
once and for all, in Jesus Christ our Lord.
Help us to hear the word clearly,
above all the other deafening voices that hammer our ears.
Help us to be obedient to that which we hear:
may we not adapt the truth to make it fit our own preconceptions,
may we not shape it into what we think it ought to be, making it fit our notions and using it to confirm our prejudices.
May we not turn the living truth into a system that pleases our sense of tidiness but ignores the questions that life thrusts at us every day.

Lord, help us to witness to the truth:
may we stand by the truth even though it invites the ridicule of others;
may we not apologise for believing what we do; in a world of ideologies, incitement to violent revolution, cynicism, emptiness, falsehood and claimant unbelief,
may we hold fast to that which has been given to us in Jesus Christ.

May we recount the truth with authority,
this word that forgives sin,
that affirms faith, hope and love,
that grants eternal life.

The world is full of walls that divide people from one another: the Berlin wall, the iron curtain, the bamboo curtain, the east-west divide, the north-south gulf, mankind torn into separate pieces. Yet on either side of every division there are Christians. And they are one in Christ . . .

An act of praise

Father, in Christ you have taken what is divided by race, temperament, colour and history and made it one. You have called people out of every nation to be your followers. Blessed be your name that, in a world where men and women are driven apart, your love unites them; in place of our hatred and suspicion you give us love, joy and peace. We thank you, Father, that we are not finally the victims of our prejudices if we open our hearts to receive your goodness.

Praying for others

Lord, we pray for your church in every part of the world, the great family of which we are a part:

we pray for those who are denied freedom in their religious beliefs,

for those called to the suffering of imprisonment, and for those few who are called to martyrdom itself:

may their courage set faith alight in other lives.

We pray for those who struggle against injustice, the men and women who have to establish love's supremacy in violent and oppressive societies:

may they be filled with your wisdom in their war against inhumanity.

We pray for our fellow Christians in the Third World,

those for whom hunger is a daily reality,

those who feel powerless to change the ways of nature or the ways of nations;

bring nearer, Lord, the day of their deliverance.

The life of prayer **Day 22**

If our prayer is an openness to God it is also an openness to life, and the more we say 'Yes' to it the more it abounds, diversifies, enriches ourselves and others and enlivens everything else. The more there is, the more there will be. The more you give, the more you receive; the more you receive, the more you have to give. *Maria Boulding*

Lord, if I am to live in the world as your servant, then it can only be as my life is open to your life.
I need to know you,
not simply by what others tell me,
nor as an idea in my head, a working hypothesis to cope with life,
nor as a simple projection of my own ideas of what God should be like:
I need to know you,
as you are,
as the God I adore,
the Friend with whom I walk,
the Lord I seek to follow,
the Life by which I live.

Lord, you come to me in prayer if only I am willing to pray:
help me to shape my life around my praying,
to order my life that prayer becomes as natural as eating and drinking, and sleeping and waking;
teach me the meaning of silence;
may I learn to listen for your voice,
hearing you even in the distractions that crowd into my mind.

Lord, help me to grow closer to you in the openness of prayer,
that I may recognise your features in the world around me,
seeing you more clearly and loving you more deeply.

The harvest of the Spirit — Day 23

The harvest of the Spirit is love, joy, peace, patience, kindness, goodness, fidelity, gentleness, and self-control. *(Galatians 5.22-23)*

Jesus promised us the Holy Spirit.
He is God at work in our lives,
releasing the possibilities that are already there
and creating new ones of which we had never dreamed.
His work in us is the work of a lifetime,
but that's not always evident in the way we think about him and speak about him:
we sometimes imagine him as the extrovert of the Holy Trinity, God in action in short, dramatic and dynamic outbursts, as if to see him were like watching a firework display;
when the Holy Spirit comes we expect
the razzamatazz of spiritual excitement,
and ecstatic invasions that seem more like a threat than a promise.
When we pray for the Holy Spirit in our lives, we should remember that a harvest doesn't explode into life, it grows . . .

God, Holy Spirit,
already you are here in my heart,
for without you I could not even turn to you or pray to you.
Your work in my life has begun before my asking.
To live without you
is to run out of strength,
to fall short of every goal,
to falter in every enterprise.

Come into my life and penetrate every part of my being,
flood every dark corner of my heart and mind with your light,
take what I already possess and shape it into the form of Christ,
give me those qualities that I lack, that I may not fail you.

Judge eternal, throned in splendour,
Lord of hosts and King of kings,
With thy living fire of judgment
Purge this realm of bitter things:
Solace all its wide dominion
With the healing of thy wings.

H. Scott Holland

Father, we offer you our thanks for the communities within which we live:

for those who accept political and social responsibility, the leaders whose decisions are so important for the welfare and happiness of those whom they lead,
for those who teach in our schools,
for those who work in our hospitals,
for those who serve in voluntary organisations, caring for the old, the handicapped, young people, and the needs of minority groups,
for those who live responsibly and peaceably with their neighbours,
for those who maintain law and make it possible for us to live our lives in a framework of order.

Father, you have called us to live our lives within the community and to accept, with our neighbours, responsibility for the happiness and well-being of our common life:

may we do so with the ardour of faith.

May we strive to make our community a place in which care, happiness, and companionship are possible,

overcoming the reserve of suburban life and the anonymity of the city.

May people feel their own worth and value,

may they be supported in their needs and provided with opportunity to grow into maturity;
may we be free of fear,
and respect one another's freedom.

Unite us in the sacred love
Of knowledge, truth, and thee;
And let our hills and valleys shout
The songs of liberty. *J.R. Wreford*

Lord, we thank you for this nation that is our home,
for this green earth that has fed us and whose beauty has delighted us,
for the traditions that have made us the people that we are,
giving us our identity and helping us to find our place within the world.

Save us, Lord, from the twin evils of a corrupted nationhood:
from the evil of racialism,
the terrible pride of race and blood that despises what is alien,
ridicules what is different,
and is blind to its own failings;
and from the opposite evil,
the evil of despising the country that gave us birth,
the cynicism that ignores the past and is pessimistic of the future,
the refusal to accept that we belong to one another.

Bless this land, Father,
reward the work of minds and hands with prosperity;
may our wealth assist others to use their resources,
may success not make us selfish,
and failure not make us desperate;
bless those who govern us,
may they accept the trust that we place in their hands,
knowing that we, the people, have delegated to them
neither our conscience nor our freedom;
strengthen our resolve to build what is good;
deliver us from tyrants and terrorists.

'The God who created the world and everything in it, and who is Lord of heaven and earth, does not live in shrines made by men. He created every race of men of one stock, to inhabit the whole earth's surface.' *(Acts 17.24,26)*

Remember in your prayers the great problems of our time: war and peace, hunger and plenty, tyranny and freedom.

War and peace
Father God, the price of peace weighs ever more heavily upon us. We turn in horror from our arsenals of destruction, but know that we have yet to find any viable alternative to meet the challenge of evil and tyranny. Too easily we forget the wars of this century and what they have taught us. We are contemptuous of the strength that has guarded the uneasy peace with which we have lived through four decades. Give us the spirit of truth as we wrestle with the agony of our time.

Hunger and plenty
Father, may those whose lands are rich remember the needs of the hungry. Let us work with our fellow-men, pooling our skills and our resources that all the earth may yield the harvest of which it is capable. May the desert of the hungry be turned into fertile land.

Tyranny and freedom
Father, may we not despise freedom nor sell it to any for the price of quiet days. Save us from committing our children to decades of oppression through our lack of vigilance and our failure of nerve. The light of freedom flickers in a chilly world. May it survive, Lord, may it survive.

What can I do?
Lord, help me to be a peace-maker, to remember the needs of others in the way I use my own resources, and to respect the freedom of other people.

Our life within the world demands that the supreme loyalty of our lives is to Christ and to his kingdom.

An act of praise

Father, we praise you for the kingdom in the midst of us:
invisible and full of divine power,
a world more real than the transient things that we see, hear and touch.
We praise you, heavenly King,
Lord above all earthly power,
for finally yours is
the kingdom, the power and the glory.

A prayer for the people of the kingdom

We ask, Lord, that what is unseen may become visible in the lives of your people:
may our actions proclaim the presence of the kingdom in the midst of the world,
may love be apparent in selfless service,
may faith be glimpsed in radical commitment to Christ and his truth,
may hope be seen in the courage and daring of the disciples of Jesus.

We ask, Lord, that the word of the kingdom may be heard in what we say:
bless the word of the preacher that it may clearly point men and women to the gate that leads to eternal life;
may the kingdom be heard
in words of reconciliation,
in words of encouragement and reassurance,
in the telling of Christ's story,
in the praise of the Church,
in the writings of theologians.

Send us, Lord, to tell everyone –
the kingdom is coming!

Nation shall not lift sword against nation
nor ever again be trained for war. *(Micah 4.3)*

Remember areas of the world known to you where there is war, division and civil strife;
pray, too, for those within your own circle of friends who are at loggerheads with each other . . .
Father, we pray for peace on earth.

We pray for those who have lived in the cockpit of war,
who have heard the crack of rifle fire,
the roar of bomb and shell,
who have been held by the clammy grip of fear,
and felt the passing brush of death.
We remember the victims of war,
those permanently disabled and disfigured,
those mentally disturbed,
those who were bereaved.
May their memories prod our sleeping minds,
may their wounds remind us of the price of our violence,
may grace heal the scar on their souls.

We pray, Father, for the victims of terrorism,
the people who have suffered at the hands of the masked murderer,
those who have been the fodder of other men's perverted dreams.
May they be steadfast in their resistance to those who use the instruments of fear and intimidation,
may they not barter the liberty that is their right,
nor come to the end of their resources.

Blessed are the peace-makers
Lord, help me to make peace between those who are divided, and not to sow seeds of dissension. May I not carry resentment and bitterness in my own heart against those who have hurt me. May I both forgive and be ready to be forgiven.

The Lord is King! child of the dust,
The judge of all the earth is just;
Holy and true are all his ways;
Let every creature speak his praise. *Josiah Conder*

A thanksgiving

Father, we thank you for the purpose you have revealed to us in Jesus our Lord. We thank you that, finally, you will set free all who are imprisoned, and bring justice for all who have been denied it, and free the world from all who treat their fellow human beings with cruelty. We thank you that the future lies with you and not with those who do what is evil.

Praying for others

Remember someone known to you by name who is a prisoner of conscience, anywhere in the world.

Pray for the work of Amnesty International and all similar organisations, that those who are wrongfully imprisoned for the sake of their conscience may be given their freedom.

Remember those countries where justice is denied to the people,
where there is no real freedom,
where people fear to speak their mind.

Remember cases of injustice known to you:
someone who was unfairly treated or wrongfully accused;
a friend whose motives were misunderstood;
someone who has been cheated.

Lord, may your justice be seen in the lives of those I have remembered before you.

A prayer for ourselves

Lord, there sometimes seems so little that I can do against the mass of injustice within the world. May I begin where I am, with these prayers that I have offered to you on behalf of others, believing that prayer changes the world. Then may I seek to live a life that is fair to others, by being generous in my judgements.

Our life in the world requires us to look for the footsteps of Jesus that in them we might place our own.

A renewal of our promises
Lord Jesus Christ, I remember with gratitude when you called me to follow you and give my life to you. I thank you that the years have not disappointed me: to follow you has been to know you, and to know you has been to love you. I remember my failings. I am conscious even now of the ways in which I have wandered from your path. Yet always you call and call again. Accept my vows again and keep me ever in your love and faith.

Asking for guidance
Lord, the questions that I face as a Christian can be so complicated. I sometimes look for clear-cut rules where there are none. Show me the way.

Praying for others
Remember those who have set out on the Christian way but failed to persist in it.
    May no sense of failure keep them from responding to Christ when he calls again.
Remember those Christians for whom confession of the name of Christ involves rejection and persecution,
    that their faith may inspire others to follow.
Remember all who hear the call of the Christ for the first time,
    that they may follow where he leads.

The prayer of St Ignatius
Teach us, good Lord,
        to serve thee as thou deservest;
        to give and not to count the cost;
        to fight and not to heed the wounds;
        to toil and not to seek for rest;
        to labour and to ask for no reward,
            save that of knowing that we do thy will;
through Jesus Christ our Lord.

In a word, there are three things that last for ever: faith, hope, and love; but the greatest of them all is love. (*1 Corinthians 13.13*)

Lord God, the world seems sometimes in danger of falling apart;
'nothing lasts for ever', we tell one another,
everything crumbles to dust;
it is a world without faith,
even faith in those things that people used to believe in — democracy, country, the inviolability of love, honour, human freedom and dignity;
it is a world without hope,
we ignore the history that has made us,
learning nothing from it,
despising the legacy it has left us,
and we fear the future and refuse to face it,
burying ourselves in the present moment;
it is a world without love,
we have talked ourselves into believing that there's nothing worth dying for,
but still believe that there are things worth killing for, our grotesque kingdoms that we seek to establish through the barrel of a gun or the blast of a bomb.

Lord, it's like trying to build at the edge of an earthquake,
the ground sways,
the fabric of life cracks,
the air is full of threat.
Lord, you have set faith, hope and love within the world and they abide:
their power of survival is infinite,
they still confront us as real options,
they still make possible what our human folly renders powerless.
May your people live by them,
without embarrassment, and with apologies to no one, may we commit ourselves to the only real alternative for the human race:
let faith, hope and love abide in us.

Advent Sunday

In all this, remember how critical the moment is. It is time for you to wake out of sleep . . . It is far on in the night; day is near. Let us therefore throw off the deeds of darkness and put on our armour as soldiers of the light. *(Romans 13.11-12)*

We thank you, Father, that your love for us is not an indulgent love that makes no demands; and for your reminders that we are accountable for what we do.

We thank you for the promise of the coming of your Son, to make us think about things we would rather not think about; to call in question the things we set our hearts on and the things we live for.

Lord, it is not so much our sins that trouble us, but our inadequacies, our failure to live that triumphant life which you promise can be ours.

Forgive us, Father, not just our failures, but some at least of our successes, because sometimes, if we are honest, we know we only succeed because we were not aiming very high in the first place. Forgive us our readiness to try for easily attainable goals, instead of the high calling to which you have called us.

Teach us, Lord, to judge ourselves, that we may not be judged by you, that at your coming we may receive your grace.

Behold, he is coming with the clouds! Every eye shall see him.
(Revelation 1.7)

I thank you, Lord, that faith is not for ever; that some day I shall see, and some day know, what now I only trust, or only hope is true.
Christ, you are our king before the world was.
Be still our king when it has ceased to be.

Bible Sunday (Second Sunday in Advent)

We thank you, Father, for the way in which the Bible can still surprise us:
that we can suddenly see new meaning in words we had read a thousand times before;
that passages which had never seemed to have much to say to us can suddenly thrill us with their significance, and scripture's driest bones come alive.

We thank you for the people whose experience is enshrined here, that, speaking different languages from us, and having different ways of life, they can still speak to us across the centuries, calling us to share their faith. We thank you that we can make their story our story, and stand beside them as your people.

We thank you for the *strangeness* of the Bible:
that it addresses itself to us in this world,
but speaks of a world beyond.
that it speaks to us in this life,
but sets our little lives in the light of eternity.

Lord, you from the beginning have not left yourself without witnesses. Teach us in their words to hear your Word;
to rejoice in its comfort,
be in awe of its judgements,
respond to its challenges,
and hope in its promises, till we no longer need to hope.

Third Sunday in Advent

We thank you, Lord, that from ancient times you sent your prophets, voices crying (all too often in the wilderness) to warn, to condemn where condemnation was needed, to appeal and to persuade, to turn the hearts of the disobedient, and to strengthen those who believed, that at your coming you might find a people prepared.

Lord, we know that you have your witnesses today. Teach us to pick out their voices from the many voices that surround us. Grant that we may not be too proud, or self-satisfied, or stubborn, to pay attention to what they say.

Our Father, our King, teach us to love your laws, that we may so walk in this world that we look forward eagerly to the coming of your Son, and enter with him into the world to come.

Fourth Sunday in Advent (Annunciation)

We thank you, Lord, for the human family into which our Lord was born, and for the faith and obedience of his parents. We thank you that he was born into a welcoming home, and that he knew the secure love of a mother and an earthly father, the mirror of your love for your children.

'Here am I,' said Mary; 'I am the Lord's servant; as you have spoken, so be it.' *(Luke 1.38)*

Lord, teach us to accept your will for us, and the part which you give us to play in your work of redeeming the world, that, whether our part be small or great, easy or difficult, our spirits may rejoice in our calling.

Lord, you have done great things for us;
give us the faith that you may do great things through us.

Christmas Eve

The preparations are over. We are ready, Lord.

Holy is your name.
Make holy our joys; holy our fellowship.
Make holy our thoughts of those absent from us; holy our memories of other years.
Be at our feast, and may your living presence enliven all we do.

Come, O Lord.

Christmas Day

We thank you, Lord, for the joys of this day:
for the joy of giving and receiving;
the joy of reunion with family and friends;
the joys of feasting and of laughter.
We thank you, Lord, for the singing of carols and Christmas hymns;
for the reading of loved and familiar words of scripture;
the joys of worship and holy celebration.

Thanks be to you, Lord, for the challenge of Christmas:
for your coming in poverty
which challenges the affluence we take for granted;
for your self-giving
which puts in perspective all our charity.

Lord, give us pause in all our celebrations to contemplate the mystery of your holy incarnation.

Father, we pray for those who at Christmas are made more aware of their own loneliness:
for those who get no presents, or very few;
for those who have no families, or whose families are far away.
We pray for those to whom Christmas brings sharp memories of happier ones.
Christ be with them and grant them consolation.

Lord of all good, your Word is in the world. Teach us to hear him, and so to celebrate his birth that we may be born again to a life of righteousness.

New Year's Eve

Lord, we offer to you the year that is past, its joys and its regrets. Sanctify our joys, and forgive our failures, for the sake of Jesus your Son.

We offer you our thanksgiving for the growth you have given us, in experience, and in grace.

Lord of the years,
we ask your blessing on the year to come.
Give us the resilience to bear its disappointments,
energy to seize its opportunities,
and openness to accept the more abundant life
which you have promised to us in Jesus Christ our Lord.

Christ, you have many services to be done.
We thank you that some are easy, some bring honour;
that in some we may please you and please ourselves.
Help us not to shirk those that are difficult or bring reproach,
in which we cannot please you except by denying ourselves.

Lord, you gave your ancient people a pillar of cloud and a pillar of fire to guide them to the place which you had promised them: guide us, too (for we have not travelled this way before), in the deserts we must pass through and the waters we must cross, that at the year's end we may be nearer to the heavenly city to which you are calling us than now at its beginning.

Epiphany

Astrologers from the east arrived in Jerusalem, asking, 'Where is the child who is born to be king of the Jews?' *(Matthew 2.1-2)*

We are glad, Lord, that these strangers were amongst your worshippers, there at the beginning. They were our representatives. Like us, they were not your people, but they recognised you. We, and they, have *become* your people; once far off, we have been brought near.

Then they opened their treasures and offered him gifts: gold, frankincense, and myrrh. *(Matthew 2.11)*

In these three gifts we offer everything: offer our wealth, our worship, and our grief.

Like them, we offer you what gifts we have.
  We bring our wisdom, such as it is;
  our skills, our talents, and our expertise.
We are sorry, Lord, that we waste so much of them on the trivial and the valueless before they ever reach your presence.
Kings, they brought their power.
  We bring our power, for we *have* power:
    power over other people;
    power to decide and plan;
    power to choose;
    power to spend.
We offer our power, knowing that we could have no power at all if it were not given us from above. Show us how to use it as you want it used.

Ash Wednesday

At that moment heaven opened; he saw the Spirit of God descending like a dove to alight upon him; and a voice from heaven was heard saying, 'This is my Son, my Beloved.' *(Matthew 3.16-17)*

Lord Jesus Christ, you were certain of your Father's call.
Give us the certainty that you have a job for us to do,
and help us to perceive what it is.
You speak to us,
through our conscience and our inner convictions;
through the voices of our fellow-Christians;
through the reading of your word;
in prayer, and in a thousand other ways.
Give us the faith to recognise your voice when we hear it,
and give us grace to answer.

Jesus was then led away by the Spirit into the wilderness, to be tempted by the devil. For forty days and nights he fasted.
(Matthew 4.1-2)

Lord, your one interest was your Father's will, so that not even hunger could distract you from your thoughts. We never apply ourselves to *anything* with that kind of intensity – not even the things we say interest us. Perhaps we have never set our minds to anything really worthy of that kind of attention. Grant us such a vision of your kingdom, and your righteousness, that the vision may control our lives.

Jesus answered, 'Scripture says, "Man cannot live on bread alone"'.
(Matthew 4.4)

Lord Jesus Christ, you are the Father's only Son,
yet you had to wrestle to know how best to do your Father's will.
You had to pray about it, think about it, looking for your answers in the Bible, as we have to do.
We thank you, Lord, that we have at our disposal all the resources which you had.
You who did all things well, show us how to serve you perfectly.

First Sunday in Lent

Save us, Lord, from the temptations that attack us through our weaknesses:

from the impulsive sin which we quickly regret;
from emotions that overpower us;
from failures of nerve and failures of determination in doing the right thing;
from failure to see things through.

Save us from the sins that we commit because we do not foresee the consequences, and from those we fall into through our muddle and inefficiency.

Save us, Lord, from the temptations that attack us through our strengths:

from using our gifts for our own ends rather than for yours;
from using our talents to impress people rather than to glorify you.

Save us from the temptation to let the gifts you have given us lie idle, instead of using them in your service and the service of our fellows.

Lord, you are able to keep us from falling; fulfil in us your promise, and present us faultless before the presence of your glory.

Second Sunday in Lent

Did *you* ever doubt, Lord?
'My God,' you said, 'why have you forsaken me?'
That sounds like doubt, more awful doubt than I have ever known.
I doubt with my head, Lord. There is a lot that doesn't make sense to me; a great deal that I cannot figure out.
Maybe doubts like that don't matter *so* much. I know that meeting you is more important than believing all the right things about you, and much more important than thinking I know all the answers.
But sometimes, Lord, you are not very real to me.
When I don't meet you, Lord, keep me going in the knowledge that you *can* be met. Keep me going, even when I don't feel your presence.
Give me the reassurance that it is worth going on.

Third Sunday in Lent

You had so little, Lord.
I have so much:
  a home,
  more money than ever *you* had,
  all kinds of modern gadgets and conveniences.
And I'm always wanting more.
  There's always something else on the list,
  that other people have, and I do not have.
You wanted nothing, but to do the will of him who sent you.

Have I got it wrong, Lord?
You put all these delightful things in the world
  for us to enjoy, didn't you?
You gave us intelligence and skill
  to invent things for our pleasure.
All the same, I don't always put first things first, do I?
Not like you did.

Fourth Sunday in Lent

Forgive me, Lord, that I am so easily satisfied.
  that I should set myself such undemanding goals,
  and be so pleased with myself about modest achievements.
Forgive me that I am so satisfied to walk,
  where you might reasonably expect that I should run, or fly.
Fill me, Lord, with faith in your promises,
  that I may undaunted contemplate your high calling,
  and press towards the goal,
    the perfection which is in Jesus Christ my Lord.

Passion Sunday

Lord of the world,
we have read our newspapers,
we have listened to the news,
and we know there is plenty of suffering in the world.
When we have to face suffering,
help us to bear it.
Give us courage to risk suffering,
and to face suffering,
when we know it is for good reasons,
as your Son Jesus suffered to do your will.
And when we cannot see the reasons,
let us know you are still there,
a hand to hold in the darkness.

Father, in some ways the sufferings of people we love are harder to bear than our own. You who sent your Son into the world know that better than we do. The hard thing is that we can do so little, that we cannot share their pain or relieve them of any of its burden.
Tell us what to say, and when to keep silent.
Show us what to do, and how to comfort.

God of all comfort, comfort us in all our afflictions, so that we may be able to comfort others with the comfort with which we ourselves are comforted by God.

Holy Week

Palm Sunday

We mean it, Lord, when we shout our hosannas.
We mean it, when we go to church to sing your praise.
We are serious when we say we want to follow you.

Sometimes we see what being a Christian is all about,
and get really excited by it.
Sometimes, when we read your word, it leaps out at us
and we really do see what it is getting at.
Sometimes we really have felt close to you in prayer.

We thank you for our moments of vision,
our moments of enthusiasm,
the times when our love for you has carried us away.

On Mondays we tend to get busy with other things.
When we are with our non-Christian friends
other interests take over.
Our enthusiasm does not get translated into loyalty
at the places where it would count most.
Our voices are not heard
at the times when they would make most difference.
To other people, Lord, all this must look like insincerity.
You know we are not insincere,
but we are inconsistent,
and weak,
and maybe cowardly.

Lord God, you who are always steadfast,
have mercy on us who falter.
Lamb of God, you who did all things well,
have mercy on us who fail.
Son of the Father, whose will is always the Father's will,
have mercy on us, who are never of a perfect mind.
You who sit at the right hand of the Father,
have mercy on us, who do not know the things that belong to our peace.

Monday before Easter (The cleansing of the temple)

Suddenly the Lord whom you seek will come to his temple . . . says the Lord of Hosts. Who can endure the day of his coming? Who can stand firm when he appears? *(Malachi 3.1)*

Lord, we thank you for your ancient temple,
and for its witness over many years,
that the dwelling-place of God is with men,
and that among their places of business and their common life,
God himself will be with them and be their God.

We praise you that there is no institution
so venerable that it may not come under your judgement,
or so holy that it may not benefit from your refining fire.

We praise you that your presence is not confined to temples made by human hands, but that you are Spirit, and that we who worship you can worship in spirit and in truth.

Holy Lord, you cleansed and renewed your temple:
cleanse and renew your Church,
that it may truly be a place of prayer for all people;
and by your presence cleanse and renew our lives,
that we may be temples of your Holy Spirit.

Tuesday before Easter (Controversies with the Jewish leaders)

You knew what conflict was, Lord,
conflicts with opponents bitter enough to murder you.
You could be angry about things that offended your Father:
you didn't mince your words.
Forgive us that we so often get angry about the wrong things,
or about quite unimportant things.
Forgive us that we save our anger for the things that hurt us,
and not for the things that offend you.
Forgive us that so much of our anger is just bad temper.
Forgive us that so often we shy away from conflict
when we should face up to it.

Show us how to face conflict in a good cause, even when it makes us unpopular or estranges us from those who would otherwise be our friends.

Lord, when we are put to the test in controversy,
then give us grace and wit to make reply.
You who were fearless,
take away our fear,
and make us strong in the cause of truth and righteousness.

Wednesday before Easter (The anointing)

Jesus said, 'Let her alone. Why must you make trouble for her? It is a fine thing she has done for me.' *(Mark 14.6)*

Lord, when clouds gather,
and tragedy looms inevitable,
and there is nothing left to do,
nothing but a gesture –
help us to see that sometimes
it is the gestures that matter most.

'She has done what lay in her power.' *(Mark 14.8)*

Maundy Thursday

Why is this night different from all other nights?

Our Lord Jesus Christ,
on this night in which he was betrayed,
broke bread with his disciples,
sharing his body and blood.
On this night,
our Lord Jesus Christ gave us new commandments,
that we love one another,
and that we keep the feast in remembrance of him.

Jesus said, 'I tell you this: one of you will betray me —one who is eating with me.' . . . One by one they said to him, 'Not I, surely?' *(Mark 14.18-19)*

Lord, forgive our complacency.

Peter said, 'Even if I must die with you, I will never disown you.' *(Matthew 26.35)*

Lord, forgive our over-confidence.

Shortly afterwards the bystanders came up and said to Peter, 'Surely you are another of them?' . . . he declared with an oath: 'I do not know the man.' *(Matthew 26.73)*

At least he was there.
Forgive us, Lord, that we do not follow you closely enough even to reach the places where the real challenges are made.

And the Lord turned and looked at Peter . . . He went outside, and wept bitterly. *(Luke 22.61-62)*

Peter must have seen that look.
He must, however fleetingly, have met his master's gaze.
He knew, and faced, what he had done.
Forgive me, Lord, that I dare not do as Peter did, and meet your gaze, and face the depth of my betrayal.

We thank you, Father, for the faith of Jesus your Son,
his readiness to do your will rather than his own,
his courage in facing what he had to face,
though in utter loneliness.
So give us of his spirit that we may share his faith,
join him in his obedience,
and receive all that he won for us by his suffering and death.

Good Friday (Words from the cross)

Jesus said, 'Father, forgive them; they do not know what they are doing.' *(Luke 23.34)*

Lord, if you, who needed no forgiveness, could forgive, how much more should we forgive, who have so much to be forgiven?

Jesus saw his mother, with the disciple whom he loved standing beside her. He said to her, 'Mother, there is your son'; and to the disciple, 'There is your mother.' *(John 19.26-27)*

Lord, in your agony you thought of the agony of others, and of your responsibility towards them. Having loved your own which were in the world, you loved them even at the end. So teach us in the worst of our distress to think not of ourselves or of our own extremity that, throughout this life, even to its last hour, we may not forget love.

And he (the criminal) said, 'Jesus, remember me when you come to your throne.' He answered, 'I tell you this: today you shall be with me in Paradise.' *(Luke 23.43)*

Lord, how small a spark of faith can kindle such a blaze of promise! This man made no great affirmation; did not even call you 'Lord'. He made no strong appeal; only 'remember me'. Jesus, our Lord, move us to such faith that we too may obtain your promises.

And about three in the afternoon Jesus cried aloud . . . 'My God, my God, why hast thou forsaken me?' *(Matthew 27.46)*

Lord, we have never been close to God as you were close to him, so we cannot guess what pain your separation from your Father caused you. But by this cry we know that you shared *our* separation, and that by sharing it you have brought us near.

After that, Jesus, aware that all had now come to its appointed end, said in fulfilment of Scripture, 'I thirst'. *(John 19.28)*

We thank you, Lord, that in your every word and deed you fulfilled the scriptures, by which we know that you were doing what your Father meant you to do. We thank you that by your obedience you have undone our disobedience, and made us acceptable to God.

Jesus drank the wine and said, 'It is finished!' *(John 19.30, GNB)*

Finished, done: the arguments, the controversies, the time for talking! Finished, ended, now, the time of pain! Finished, indeed, the work that you had to do! You have done everything for our salvation.

Then Jesus gave a loud cry and said, 'Father, into thy hands I commit my spirit.' *(Luke 23.46)*

Make us, Lord, like you, content to do our work and leave the outcome to another. Into the hands of your Father, and our Father, we commit ourselves: our life and our death, our present and our future, both in this world and in eternity.

Good Friday evening

It is all over — the hardest of deaths.
It is finished.
The soldiers have gone off duty,
the sightseers have dispersed,
the show is over.

What did they see?
  A man — three men in all — being tortured to death.
  A gruesome political murder.
They saw, and did not see,
  the Son of Man being lifted up to draw all men to him;
  the Lamb of God being sacrificed, taking away the sin of the world.
They saw, but did not see,
  how God so loved the world that he gave his only Son.
They saw, but did not see,
  how God was in Christ reconciling the world to himself.

Lord, as we meditate on the suffering of your Son, show us the face of God behind the tortured human face, that we may see the tortured human face behind the face of God. Make real to us, as we can bear it, the human agony of this day; so may we perceive the divine glory.

Easter Day

This is the day on which the Lord has acted;
let us exult and rejoice in it. *(Psalm 118.24)*

Lord, help us to remember your resurrection not only on this one day in the year, but to celebrate it every Sunday; and indeed to remember every day and every hour that we live in you and that you live in us.

If then you have been raised with Christ, seek the things that are above, where Christ is, seated at the right hand of God.
(Colossians 3.1, RSV)

Lord Jesus, when your Father raised you from the dead,
he did it not only for your sake,
but for ours.
Your resurrection is not just something that happened to *you*,
but that happens to *us*.
Teach us what it means to share your resurrection.
Grant us your new life *now*,
that we may seek the things that are above,
and live here the life of heaven.

Lord Jesus Christ, you have made all things new.
Let your new light shine upon us.
Sun of righteousness,
cause your face to shine on us,
and bring us healing.

Easter evening

He took bread and said the blessing; he broke the bread, and offered it to them. Then their eyes were opened, and they recognised him; and he vanished from their sight. *(Luke 24.31)*

Lord, we do not see your bodily form. Give us such faith that we do not need to see. Teach us to see you in the opening of the scriptures, and to know your presence in the breaking of the bread.

Ascension Day

Lift up your heads, you gates,
lift yourselves up, you everlasting doors,
that the king of glory may come in.
Who is the king of glory? *(Psalm 24.7-8a)*

You are the king of glory, O Christ; you are the everlasting Son of the Father. *(Te Deum)*

We thank you, Lord, that you have not gone away, but that you are here more than ever.

We praise you because your work on earth is completed:
the holy mystery of your incarnation,
baptism, fasting and temptation,
agony and bloody sweat,
cross and passion,
death and burial,
resurrection —
all are over; once, and for all.
Your triumph is complete;
a triumph visible, though not to all.
We bless you that you have opened the kingdom of heaven to all believers.
What you have done, you have done for us.
What you have won, you have won for us.

Risen and ascended Lord, teach us to set our minds on things that are above, where you are, seated at the right hand of God, so that when you appear, we also may appear with you in glory.

Pentecost

You promised us power, Lord.
Power is certainly what we need.
We do not lack good intentions, Lord.
    We can see quite clearly
    all sorts of things that we ought to be doing,
    things we know would please you.
    But most of them do not get done.
Give us the energy, the energy of your Spirit.
Give us the will, Lord.
Give us the new heart you have promised.

We have some idea of the sort of people you want us to be.
Sometimes we feel we are making progress,
    but mostly we know we are falling a long way short.
We try,
    but trying does not seem to be enough.
Take hold of us, Lord.
    Take us over.
        Help us to get it into our heads
        that trusting you is the answer, not trying.
We are yours, Lord; take possession of us.

Lord Holy Spirit, we thank you for your promise to set us free:
    free from timidity,
    free to begin again,
        not disillusioned by our past failures and mistakes;
    free to be ourselves, our real selves,
        the selves which the Creator meant us to be;
    free to accomplish those things that you want done.
Grant us now the openness of heart,
    the self-forgetfulness,
        to claim your promise and accept your freedom.

Trinity Sunday

I can't *explain* you, Lord.
    But you being what you are,
    and I being what I am,
    that doesn't surprise me.
What I have learnt about you makes a kind of sense,
    but I haven't got it all worked out.
Lord God, you made me, and everything else that is,
    or ever was, or ever will be.
        That's an idea I can get hold of.

You are my Father,
    and the Father of us all;
        your care and love are something we can all depend on.
            That comforts me.
Your Son, Jesus, I know about.
    I can grasp that his work is your work;
    that when he died for us, that was your love displayed;
    that when I face his challenge, that is your challenge.
    When I meet him, I am meeting you.
Your Holy Spirit I know something about — not enough.
    When I feel his power in me, that is your power.

This is no explanation, Lord, but a description of how it seems to me, how I encounter you.

I thank you Lord, Father, Son and Holy Spirit, that faith is not a matter of knowing the right formulas or putting things into the right words, but of knowing what you have done for me, and being willing to let you work through me and in me; of letting your love control me.

Lord, give me that kind of faith.

OCCASIONAL PRAYERS

The Seasons

An autumn day

Blessed are you, O Lord our God, king of the universe:
you have made every season with its virtues proper to it.
We thank you that there is a time to die as well as a time to be born,
and that you have made everything beautiful in its time.
Blessed are you, O Lord,
who remind us in the glory of this season
that there is triumph in death,
and that we must die to live again.

A winter day

We thank you, Lord, for the brightness of winter sun;
for winter's work, and winter's entertainments;
for the warmth of home, and all its comforts.

Lord of all times and all seasons,
we thank you that there is no season without its satisfactions, and that there is no time without its promises.

Lord, when we have no light, show us the treasures of darkness.

A spring day

Lord, we are creatures of time; the passing of the seasons is dear to us. We welcome the spring as a familiar friend, and yet its newness always takes us by surprise. We never get used to your blessings, Lord. In every season they are better than we remembered. Your gifts, however often we receive them, still outstrip our anticipations.

Unchanging Lord, you are the same, yesterday, today and for ever: in your sight even the mountains and the seas are transient things. Daily you roll away the light from before the darkness and the darkness from before the light; yet you are the same: in you is no variableness, neither shadow of turning.

Eternal Lord, grant that while we delight in seasons and changing years, we may rejoice in the comfort that you hold us in everlasting arms.

A summer day

For long days and warm evenings,
for sun, and for afternoons in gardens,
  we thank you, Lord.
For cool drinks and summer salads,
for relaxation and summer games,
  we thank you, Lord.
For summer holidays and summer outings;
for opportunities to see new places,
and to renew acquaintance with familiar ones,
  we thank you, Lord.
For time to reflect, to renew energies, to plan ahead,
  we thank you, Lord.
For summer's work as well as summer leisure,
for summer storms as well as summer stillness,
  we thank you, Lord.

Lord of the year, and Lord of years, all times are in your hand; seasons of growth, seasons of refreshment, seasons of waiting, and seasons of fruition, are all from you.
Lord, you have given us time. Move us so to use it that we may apprehend eternity.

Harvest festival

Lord, we offer you all we have produced this year:
  the things that we have made in factories;
  the figures we have produced in offices;
  the crops grown in fields and gardens.
We have maintained the fabric of the world, Lord. This is your work.

Lord, some of us have not made anything (except money),
  but we have organised, administered, managed,
  taken decisions, got things done.
We have helped to make and maintain order. This is your work.

Lord, we offer you the work we have done at home:
  the meals made, the clothes washed, the cleaning done,
  the decorating, the gardening, the odd jobs.
We have produced beauty or decency, tidiness and efficiency. This is your work.

Lord, you have created things, made things, ordered things, caused things to grow, and you take satisfaction in all that you do. We thank you that you have made us in your image.

On taking up a new job

Lord God, you made me,
you know what is in me;
you put me where I am.
Make me flexible enough to learn new skills and new attitudes,
without forgetting what experience has taught me already.
Help me to pay attention to what other people are saying to me,
and yet to know my own mind.
Make me ready to learn from anyone,
and ready to help anyone learn.
Make me ready to accept responsibility when it is offered,
and ready to share responsibility when it is appropriate.
Let me not be too quick to jump to conclusions;
let me not be too slow to ask advice.
Help me to work conscientiously,
to listen patiently,
to think clearly,
to decide firmly,
and to do everything as if in your presence.

On a child's starting school

Teach me to let go, Lord:
to let my child take his own steps into the big world,
to watch, and care, but to let him grow,
as you, Lord, let us all grow,
all of us, your children.
You let us make our own choices, our own mistakes,
although you love us — *because* you love us.
Lord, give me the love that has confidence,
the love that trusts.
My child is your child, too.
You, too, are his Father.
He is ours, Lord, yours and mine; upheld by both our loves.
We both want the best for him.
Let him be sure of that, now and wherever he goes.

A holiday

Lord, you have given us these days,
these hours,
this freedom,
this world to be happy in,
with all its possibilities.

Thanks be to you.

Be with us in relaxation or activity,
in calmness or excitement,
in the crowd, and when we are alone.
Keep us from any selfishness in our enjoyment,
and let our happiness be pure.

A wedding

Lord, what a cheerful, serious thing a wedding is!
We thank you that we can share it.

God, you are love, for you have told us so.
You have put love in our very nature,
and when we love each other we are most like you.
Give those who make their promises today
the strong, determined love that does not fail.

We thank you that today we share what is in essence such a private happiness. The love is theirs, the promises are theirs, yet our love, too, supports them.
Lord, as the gifts that we have brought
help to build up their home,
may all our hopes and wishes, and our prayers
be bound into its fabric.

Pay day

Blessed are you, O Lord, for you have given us sufficient for our needs. Teach us how to dispose what you have given us:
to spend, and get pleasure out of spending, but not to squander;
to spend with carefulness, but not anxiety;
and not to envy what we cannot afford.
Let us so learn faithfulness in the things of this world
that we may be faithful in the greater things of your kingdom,
and at last be received into eternal habitations.

A disappointment

Blessed are you, O Lord!
You have made me.
Everything I have, you have given me.
All things depend on you,
and all your creation gives you praise.
Lord, you know how I feel.
I am not trying to persuade myself that I don't care.
I do care, and I am disappointed.
I am asking you to help me face this,
not to pretend it isn't there.
Lord, help me not to be a worse person because of what has happened,
but a better one.
That is what matters most to me,
and I know it is what matters most to you.
What other people are concerned in this?
What are their feelings?
Lord, help me to pray for them.
Remind me of your blessings, Lord.
In spite of my disappointments, what remains to me?
Remind me, not so that I can pretend I have lost nothing important, but to put it in perspective.
What disappointments and disasters have I been spared?
Blessed are you, O Lord,
for all you have done for me, and in me.
Lord, my Father, you want the best for me:
show me how to be the best I can, for you.

On listening to music

Lord of all joy,
all pure joy comes from you,
and all pure joy ascends to you like prayer.
Blessed are you, for all our earthly music
is but an echo of the song sung at creation,
or fragments anticipated of the new song of heaven.

On being out of work

Thank you, Lord, because you made me, with my talents, such as they are, my skills — all my capacities. You didn't mean them to lie around unused. Show me where I can use them.

Thank you, Lord, because with all your other gifts you gave me resilience, a certain toughness of spirit. Show me how to make the adjustments that I have to make.

Father, I know that whatever happens to me, however unwelcome, there is always something to be learnt from it. What do you want me to learn from this experience? Show it to me.

And make me sure of this: that neither death nor life, principalities nor powers, employment nor unemployment can separate me from your love, which is shown to me in Christ Jesus my Lord.

On arranging flowers

Someone else planted these flowers, Lord.
Someone else grew them,
  gave them the attention they needed.
I have done nothing,
  but take them, and place them here.
    That is my response to their beauty:
    the beauty which you have bestowed on them.
That is my worship of you who created them.

Blessed are you, O Lord our God, who have made flowers to grow from the earth.
Lord of the world, you have lavished such splendour on such transient things. How great must be the splendour of the things which stand for ever!

On not being able to pray

I can't pray, Lord.
The thoughts will not come.
The feelings are just not there.
But your Son is praying.
I have your word for that.
He is praying for me, much better than I could ever pray for myself.
Let me just say this, Lord —
let me say 'Yes' to his prayers.
Whatever he is asking on my behalf,
'Yes' to that, 'Amen' to that.
Angels and archangels are all around, Lord, and all the company of heaven. I cannot see them. I do not feel them here. But count their prayers as my prayers, their praise as mine. And let my silence be lost in their perpetual alleluias.

A prayer before Holy Communion

I thank you, Lord, that you have given to us your people, commandments that are not too hard for us, and for this simplest of all commands: 'Take, eat.'
As I am faithful in this small obedience,
so make me faithful in all things.
Lord, give me grace
to do what you command,
to accept what you offer,
to know what you have done for me,
and to receive your life into myself.
Blessed are you, O Lord our God, king of the universe,
for you have given us the bread of life.

A wet day

Your mercy, Lord, soaks the earth:
the grass, the trees, the growing crops rejoice in it.
They have no umbrellas to fend off your grace.